BEDROCK FOR WEDLOCK

A compendium for singles, searching, engaged, trouble home and married.

Daramola Joel Odunayo

Tel: 08033275896, 07028206482

ISBN: 9798368203669

Published by
CHRIST THE REDEEMER'S MINISTRIES
1-9, Redemption Way, P.M.B. 1088, Ebute Metta, Lagos, Nigeria.

Unless otherwise stated, all scriptural quotation are from the Authorized King James Version of the Holy Bible.

Printed in Nigeria by: **CRM PRESS**
KM 46 Lagos-Ibadan Expressway, CRM Shopping Complex, Back of Old Auditorium, Redemption Camp,
Tel: 08077833792, 08069452037
E-mail: crmpress@yahoo.com

Table of Contents

DEDICATION

This book is dedicated to our Lord Jesus Christ; my Saviour and the Holy Spirit my senior partner in life and ministry and my heavenly Father, the Almighty God (YAHWEH) and to my father in the Lord,

Pastor E. A. Adebayo And to my lovely wife Pastor Mrs. Oluseyi Christiana Daramola for our 21st wedding anniversary also to everyone that attends 'Power Service' our weekly breakthrough and deliverance service in various locations.

ACKNOWLEDGEMENT

I appreciate the efforts of everybody who at different stages contributed immensely to the success of this book.

Also my sincere regards and appreciation go to my better half who helped me in typing the book, and Pastor Mrs. C O Daramola for her selfless work who took time to read the manuscript and make very useful adjustment, Pastor Aremu Adegoke of CRM press that help in proof reading and many others that help to bring the dream come to reality.

Bedrock 1: MARITAL AFFAIR *IS* MARRIAGE AFFAIR

THE SCHOOL CALLED MARRIAGE:

Marriage is the only school where you get a certificate before you start. It is also a school where you will never graduate. It's a school without a break or a free period.
It is a school where no one is allowed to drop out.
It is a school you will have to attend every day of your life. It is a school where there is no sick leave or holidays. It is a school founded by God on the foundation of love. The walls are made out of trust. The doors made out of acceptance. The windows made out of understanding. The furniture is made out of blessings and the roof made out of faith.

Be reminded that you are just a student in the school and not the principal. God is the principal and even in times of storm, do not be unwise. Keep in mind that this school is the safest place to be. Never go to sleep before completing your assignments for the day. Do not forget to communicate with your classmate and with the Principal. If you find out something in your classmate (spouse) that you do not appreciate, remember your classmate is also just a student not a graduate. God is not finished with him/her yet; so take it as a challenge and work on it together.

Do not forget to study the Holy Book (the main textbook of this school). Start each day with a sacred assembly and end it the same way. Sometimes you will feel like not attending classes, yet you have to. When tempted to quit; find courage and continue. Some tests and exams may be tough but remember the Principal knows how much you can bear and yet it is a school better than any other.

It's one of the best schools on earth where joy, peace and happiness accompany each lesson of the day. Different subjects are offered in this school, yet love is the major subject. After all the years of theorizing about it, now you have a chance to practice it.

To be loved is a good thing, but to love is the greatest privilege of them all. Marriage is a place of love, so love your spouse. The Almighty God will give you the grace to love your spouse.

DEEP THOUGHT

Marriage is a life sentence. Permit me to say that if love is blind, marriage is an institution for the blind. Marriage is an institution in which a man loses his Bachelor Degree and the woman gets her Masters. Marriage is full of excitement and frustrations. In the first year of marriage, the man speaks and the woman listens. In the second year, the woman speaks and the man listens. In the third year, they both speak and the neighbours listen.
Getting married is like going to the restaurant with friends. You order what you want, and when you see what the other fellow ask…you wish you had ordered that instead.

Marriage is a school where one learns very late. For an ideal marriage, the man should be deaf while the woman is blind. It is not the lack of love but the lack of friendship that ends marriage. If you don't like loneliness, then don't get married because in marriage sometime it can be lonely. We are blinded by love but our eyes are opened by marriage. *At a cocktail party, one woman said to another… "Are you not wearing your ring on the wrong finger?" The other replied, 'Yes, I am. I am married to the wrong man.'*

It doesn't matter how often a married man changes his job, he still ends up with the same boss. When a man opens the door of his car for his wife, you can be sure of one thing –either the car is new or the wife is. Marriage is the best thing that can ever happen to a man, if he marries right.

Bedrock 2: MARRIAGE FOUNDATION

"And the LORD God said; it is not good that the man should be alone; I will make him a help mate for him." Genesis 2:18.

A house is where you live and a home is where you belong. A man builds a house but a woman makes a home. Building a home is similar to building a physical structure and the most crucial aspect of the two is the foundation. After you locate the site, be ready to build a rugged and time enduring foundation.

The foundation upon which you build your marriage relationship is *mutually agreeable and binding*. It is a *life-time commitment where cooperation is essential.*

Is your partnership built on this foundation?

Just as teammates have to go into a game with the same plan, you and your partner must approach your marriage not with the attitude of 'me versus you,' but with the attitude of being *fully committed to the same plan.*

Nobody gets married without the highest of hopes that this is going to be one of the finest, friendliest, most congenial and most satisfying relationships that anybody ever had. However, we need to stop and consider what goes into a relationship that will guarantee happiness, contentment and satisfaction.

Sometimes it seems as though a long-lasting marriage is determined by chance or circumstances or just plain old luck. However, there are some steps that will enable you to establish your marriage on a solid foundation that will help you stay in it for the long haul.

TERMS IN MARRIAGE

Marriage is a life union between a man and a woman in fulfilment of the law of the Lord. It is a permanent vow which should not be tampered with except by death.

Marriage is a legal relationship between spouses: a legally recognized relationship established by a civil or religious ceremony between two people who intend to live together till death do them part. Marriage involves leaving and cleaving. It is a one-flesh relationship and it is for the matured.

Marriage is a one-way institution. Way you go into it: it is very difficult for you to return because it is a one way drive traffic.

Marriage is the only institution you don't graduate from and that is why you need to understand marriage before you go into it Amos 3:3.

The man and wife belong to the same spiritual kingdom in the realm of the soul, both of them should have the same mind concerning various matters, especially the principles of the doctrine of Christ as stated in Heb.6:1-2. Two people cannot walk together except they agree Amos 3:3. You both must accept the fact that your bodies belong to each other and must be ready to share it with one another. Scripturally, this union is for a life time. It should therefore, not to be entered into without due consideration. It is important to know what it is all about before one says "I do"

In Genesis 2:18-25, we saw God initiating the idea of a male and female relationship, in which both could succour one another. Marriage was founded by God to provide help that is suitable, adaptable and complementary to establish unity and for procreation.

The marriage covenant has some conditions that must be fulfilled before the benefits can be enjoyed. The man has to love and the woman must submit to her husband and they both must bring up their children in the fear of the Lord.
Marriage is not peculiar to any culture or country of the world; it is heaven's culture. It is therefore not traditional in any way, but scriptural. God's word gives us guidance on what need to be known about it in order to make it successful. Since Marriage was instituted by God Himself, anyone who wants to succeed in marriage should make God the centre of such a relationship. God is the only sure foundation for success in marriage.

The primary purpose of marriage is not to please you, but to serve God. God wants us to be happy, but being "happy" is subject to so many variances and circumstances.

The book of Genesis recorded the account of how God created Eve as a helpmeet to help Adam perform his duty in the garden to have dominion over the earth. That is God's purpose for marriage – a team fulfilling God's call together, pleased with each other, but primarily focused on Him and not their own pleasure.

So to have a successful marriage, the most important thing is to ensure that you follow the principles that He laid down when He designed marriage. The irony is, when we focus on His principles instead of our pleasures, we end up having a very satisfying and pleasant marriage.

The Dos and Don'ts in Marriage

You are expected not to commit fornication before marriage. Both the man and the woman should be committed to the marriage. No one should lord it over the other. Don't defraud one another. Don't allow Satan to tempt you so pray and fast and above all divorce is not allowed by God.

Many times people wishing to get married come to me and say they have four people they are interested in and they wish to know the will of God. This always places me in a crossroad, as the doctrines of my denomination says we should never choose for anyone, but ask them to speak on the vision they saw, even if you see or know a preferred one.

In Ezekiel 14:4, 9-10, we are made to understand that if you come prepared with a choice to a prophet, and you ask him to choose for you, the answer will be as delusive as the choice already made. So if a man with three choices of women for marriage comes; let's call them Deborah, Kemi and Vivian and he loves Vivian more than the other two, and he goes to any prophet, they will tell him Vivian is the best. Why? Because he has already set his love on one and he would not be given a contrary answer.

Imagine if the man took the three names to the pastor, and he said, 'I think you love one', your next answer would be, 'Sir, you are just right. That's Sister Vivian.' It is your mind. So now how do you receive from God?

In Jer. 8:7-11, the bible tells us that: Truly, the stork in the heavens is conscious of her fixed times; the dove and the swallow and the crane keep to the times of their coming; but my people have no knowledge of the law of the Lord. How is it that you say, we are wise and the law of the Lord is with us? But see, the false pen of the scribes has made it false. The wise men are shamed, they are overcome with fear and taken: see, they have given up the word of the Lord; and what use is their wisdom to them? So I will give their wives to others, and their fields to those who will take them for themselves: for everyone, from the least to the greatest, is given up to getting money; from the priest even to the prophet, everyone is false. And they have made little of the wounds of the daughter of Zion, saying, Peace, peace; when there is no peace.

God says here that even the birds of the air know the season, but we humans use formulae. You must know that what it does is simply to mislead you.

I remember when I was searching for a wife; I bought many books to learn so many things. I remember one of the materials I read was written by Pastor Kumuyi of the Deeper Life Bible Church. He talked about how some people use mental standpoints to reason out things. The most common is to put out what is called a fleece. When putting out a fleece, the individual prays something like this: "Lord, if you want me to do this—then you do that." Or, "God, if you want me to do this, then let that happen." Or to discover their wife, "Lord, if I throw this coin up and it is tail, I will go for that one, and if it is head, I will go for the other one." The devil may turn the tail, because you are in his territory

Marriage councillors, whether Christian or secular, will even tell you that 99% of marital problems arises because a husband or wife (or both) have not seen himself/herself or themselves as unique and worthy individuals. In other words, they have a bad self-image, or they are schizophrenic in some way and not whole, or they are not separate but always depend on some other person to make them happy.

What are the hindrances to finding a spouse?

Some people fast and pray without results. This does not mean God has stopped listening to prayers. It is simply that when he speaks, many do not listen like we mentioned earlier. So what we will be doing here is to know when God speaks to us and how to listen to him when he does.

Don't be deceived you can't be enjoying sin partners (boyfriends and girlfriends) or abusing and breaking the heart of many in the name of used and dump and still expect God to get you best spouse

Curses

There are some who are under one form of curse or the other. I pray that by the time you finish reading this book, you shall be delivered in Jesus Name.

There was a case of a sister. She was born again even baptised by immersion, but she was under a curse. When I was praying, God asked me to call her and speak to her. It happened that when she was in the secondary school, she was in a relationship with someone, but when she moved away from the town; she became born again so when she returned to her town, she told the brother that she would not be able to go on with the relationship again. The brother was infuriated and said to her, 'you will never find a husband.' Since that time, no one has asked for her hand in marriage, until we prayed for her and revoked the curse.

Interpersonal Relationship

A Curse is to be tackled and taken seriously, but there are other reasons that we do not take notice of and that is interpersonal relationship. There are some sisters who frown so that people would know that they are spiritual. There could a man who is interested in them but they are afraid of their constant disposition.

Are you the type who would not extend your hands for hand shake? These things as minor as they seem, count because it would mean you are unfriendly and unreceptive. No one wants a 'fighter-looking spouse'.

Appearance

When we talk about appearance, we are not talking about beauty or anything like that but your mode of dressing. There is a popular saying that goes thus: 'dress the way you want to be addressed.' Anyone who comes to the church in skimpy dresses or even goes around town in such would be viewed as irresponsible or your dress is too extravagant that it makes people to believe you are too costly.

Then there are those who go about claiming to be Christians and go about looking dirty and shabby. There is no reason to look pathetic because you want to claim that you know Christ.

Before I got married, I know that at least a man look out for certain things in a woman. No man likes a shabby looking woman. There was a lady in the church, who in the name of fasting and praying ended up looking like a hag. I told her to begin to take blood tonic. You can pray anyhow, but precaution must be taken in fasting, so that you don't end up looking worse than the problem you are praying for. This is not saying fasting is bad, but you must not convince yourself into believing that your ability to fast for long hours or days is the breakthrough you need.

The book of 2Timothy 2:19 says: *'Nevertheless the foundation of God standeth sure, having this seal; The Lord knoweth them that are his. And, Let everyone that nameth the name of Christ depart from iniquity.'* Stand on God's promise; it is the sure way. Apply God's method and do not choose for God.

There was a brother in one of our parishes, who made a remark at our national youth convention in 1994. He said that God is the blacksmith of heaven, but we humans insist on choosing our own iron for him to bring out a shape for us. Our G.O. answered that God would use the iron (for the one who insists on his way) and the individual would manage it for the rest of his life and pray for God's grace to see them through but those who wait for the right iron to be used can face any battle.

Inspiration by revelation

God gave me an illustration using a car. He said when people want to buy a car, we all have our preferences. Some like a Mercedes Benz because it is fashionable, some like Honda for its roominess. He said many people have preferences because of their personal taste and not because of the durability of the product.

There was a time I was going to buy a car and I found out that I needed something that would carry my tools. At that point, I needed a car that was durable for that purpose and not just for comfort. My tool is my asset so I needed something durable. It is the same for someone getting married. You need a spouse who is durable – someone who can stand with you and would not give up.

There was a story of a couple. The wife came from a very rich background, but there was this persistent migraine which the wife usually had that could not be cured, until someone gave her a charm to keep under her bed. At the time they were going to marry, the woman's parents resisted, because the man came from a poor background. However, the wife simply said, 'the only thing that interest her is if he will be willing to carry her liability.' All she needed was for him to live through the rigours of her migraine and be willing to live with the charm with her.

For a long time, he and his wife lived with this charm until one day they went to the Redemption Camp and Pastor E. A. Adeboye was preaching and he said, 'There's someone here who has had migraine for so-so-so years,' and he prayed for the person. The issue is that, he was willing to bear his wife's burden. How many of us can carry our own burden, let alone another person's? There are many people who are not ready to carry any liability; so one week after the wedding, they are divorced.

There was the case of a brother living in the same house with us who married at the age of thirty-nine, yet eight (8) days after the wedding, his wife slapped him and from then trouble started. This was someone who got married in the church, yet he married wrongly. On the day his wife left him, he danced all day.

When you are about to get married, look for someone who is willing to take responsibility or liability that may arise.

The bible recorded the following account in Genesis 2: 18-24. *"And the LORD God said, It is not good that the man should be alone; I will make him an help meet for him. And out of the ground the LORD God formed every beast of the field, and every fowl of the air; and brought them unto Adam to see what he would call them: and whatsoever Adam called every living creature that was the name thereof. And Adam gave names to all cattle, and to the fowl of the air, and to every beast of the field; but for Adam there was not found an help meet for him. And the LORD God caused a deep sleep to fall upon Adam, and he slept: and he took one of his ribs, and closed up the flesh instead thereof; And the rib, which the*

LORD God had taken from man, made he a woman, and brought her unto the man. And Adam said,
This is now bone of my bones, and flesh of my flesh: she shall be called Woman, because she was taken out of Man. Therefore shall a man leave his father and his mother, and shall cleave unto his wife: and they shall be one flesh".

When you are ready to marry, you will be surprised that all sorts of people will come. Many of them are simply distractions and not the real one.

From the bible verses above, God formed creatures and brought them to Adam, who named them but found no suitable helpmate but when Eve came, he knew. He said, 'this is the bone of my bones.' It was an instant attraction that was genuine and true, because they were suited for each other. God did not say this is your wife, but immediately he saw her, he said, 'yes!' So who *chooses* for a man? Is God still choosing for people?

There are many schools of thought that think God has stopped choosing for man. I will tell you a story of Jacob as an example. When he was ready to marry, God chose Leah for him, but he loved Rachel. God saw that she (Rachel) loved idols and would become barren, even though she was pretty. He served another seven years to get his beloved and he did not even enjoy her for long.

You see when God chooses for you, he might bring someone who is not in the light of what you have in mind, but it is the best. Many people are led by their thought and already have an idea of what they want. However, is your desire in line with God's desire?

There are people who having waited long they think that God does not desire that they marry, but I tell you if God does not wish that to happen, he would have spoken to you. The only person who is mentioned being single in his life time is Apostle Paul but he said that it is 'better to marry than to remain single and get involved in immoral act.' God wants you to marry. For every brother there is a sister. There are hindrances but we must leave our spiritual ego and physical ego. Do not marry because someone is handsome or beautiful.

A pastor friend told me a story of a sister in her church. She was thirty-six years and unmarried. At that time, there was a brother who joined the church and he was always eager to do anything there. In just seven months, he was baptised. There was nothing he was not willing to do. Then one day, he told the pastor that he saw a vision that the sister is his wife. The pastor prayed and concluded that the man was not God's choice for her. He told the sister that he saw him as a demon. The sister took the matter to the elders in the church and they began to abuse the pastor, saying he was too selfish. Why would he not want the woman to marry? Finally, he succumbed.

It happened that few months after the wedding, the sister began to grow lean. Whenever they asked her what was wrong, she said nothing. One day, the pastor called her into the office and said whatever happened, she must talk. The sister burst into tears and told him a baffling story. At that point, she said she didn't care if she died, because the man said the day she revealed the secret she would die. Now, it happened that her husband would at night turn into a monkey and make love with her until daybreak. The man was a member of a cult, and they turned into monkey every night to become rich.

When she finished the story, the pastor told her they would stay in that office and wait until God answer them. They began to cry and pray. After two hours God answered them and said he had forgiven her, because the only thing they prayed for was forgiveness. Seven days after, the brother died. The death that should have been the woman's was put on the man's head. You see, some people are in human flesh, but they are possessed by demons. It is better for you to know than not to know.

A member of my former parish introduced one sister to me for prayer. We both prayed concerning the brother, God never told me that they belong to each other but this girl insisted that he was born again, even a minister in a prominent Pentecostal church. But I told her that he was not good for her. After a lot of disagreement, I sent her to my Provincial Pastor then. She convinced him and later got married to the man. They were married in April and separated in May that same year.

I also had my own experience of the first lady i thought would marry; we both went to the pastor several times and the only thing he said which made me to change my mind was 'Pray o!' I know that in the Redeemed Christian church of God, once you are given such words and no more is said; then you really need to hands off. It was a thousand words spoken to express that there was a heavy log on that route.

I am glad I broke off from the relationship, even though I waited several years before I met my wife. It was after we broke the courtship that I learnt of the many things she did. You see, some people once you are in a relationship they would take your name to a white garment church or herbalist to see your future.

There was a brother, who told me that if he wanted a woman, all he needed to do was to put honey on paper and write the name of the lady on it, say some certain words and read some

Psalms and he would walk to the woman he desired and get her. *What if she turns to be a witch?*

You see, the mere fact that a born again comes to you does not mean it is the will of God for you. Even if the Pastor brings his brother or sister and says, 'this is my relative, marry him' that never proves that this is God's will. You remember again, when Adam saw Eve, he knew her.

WHO SHOULD WE MARRY?

1. **MARRY YOUR FRIEND.**
   One who is faithful to you, who can respect you even while correcting you, who edifies your spirituality and character, who nourishes your spirit, soul and body and who can defend you in your absence

2. **MARRY A GOD-FEARING PERSON.**
   Not just a good person but a God- fearing person who is born again and has the fear of God, who carries the presence and Grace of GOD, who challenges you to improve in your work and walk with God, someone who is accountable to his/her Pastor and the one who submits and can be changed by the Word of God.

3. **MARRY SOMEONE WHO UNDERSTANDS YOU.**
   Especially your temperament, your purpose, your love language, your weaknesses, your gift and talents and your needs

4. **MARRY SOMEONE WHO WANTS TO GROW WITH YOU.**
   Someone who accepts you, for who you are, not a person who wants to change everything about you, someone who is interested in becoming a better friend and someone who

works on his/her weaknesses and accepts that you are not perfect.

It is good to marry your friend; that is, someone who you agree with. Amos 3: 3 says, *'Can two work together, except they agreed?'* That brings us to ethnicity. Can a Yoruba man marry an Igbo woman? The answer is yes; but there would be maturity and understanding.

There was a woman who after giving birth, her mother-in-law asked her not to eat salt and pepper for seven days. She said it was their culture. In marrying from a different background, one must have a spiritual, physical and emotional information and maturity to handle them if not I will advise don't venture into such a relationship.

In this case little can your church do but for you to understand their culture, tradition background and get information of his/her upbringing. *A man who is still under the control of his parents is not ready for marriage*

What can a man living in his father's house say or do? A man who is under control cannot understand the things around him because he would have say no to the things that can be avoided. A man living under his parents and depending on them for day-to-day feeding cannot decide if he would not want alcohol served at his wedding. Genesis 2:24-25. Separate from your parents first.

WHO SHOULD A CHRISTIAN MARRY?

A Christians should only marry a Christians. II Cor.6:14-17. A Mature single, a responsible widow or widowers, a person in your faith, who you are compatible with, someone whose background, health, spirituality, career/vocation and calling you can handle.

If you want to marry someone older than you; age is not a barrier. So if the age difference is just one or two years, then it is fine. One thing about marriage is that, once you are married, you ought to become age mates. This is because, the bible says, *'two must become one.'* In any case, the wife must be submissive.

Which age did the Bible give as age for marriage?

Anyone less than twenty should not think of marriage. Several people in the bible married at 30. In this modern times however, we may say, 22-25 for women and 25-27 for men. For many who marry late, you have to understand that sometimes, God puts you through some circumstances because he has a bigger plan for you.

One other reason, marriage is encouraged early these days, is to avoid fornication. But we must always remember that, marrying at a younger age can cause **In vitro fertilization (IVF).**

Sometimes God can give you someone you don't love physically or at first? Like if you desire a tall person and he gives you a short man. God can do that. He knows you better than anyone, so he'll give you exactly what you need.

DO A RESEARCH ON YOUR FUTURE PARTNER.

Find out where is he/she is from? Is he/she known in the church? Has he impregnated other people before? Do people marry well in his/her family? Do they have any bad history of mental ailment? Etc. You need to do a search because different kinds of spouse exist, you also need to be wise because fake men and women abound.

Searching and finding are necessary because of suitability. Not everyone is suitable or right for your purpose. Remember that when you are searching; these facts are extremely important:

First, the woman is made for the man (Help meet). Look for a partner who can help you. Also have a vision before you propose (accept when he has a vision).

In addition never marry if he can't take care of himself when it is obvious that he has no means of Livelihood.

While searching; endeavour to submit to God, seek Pastoral counsel, get parental consent and be courteous

WHAT DO WE DO WHEN WE BOTH FIND OURSELVES?

Set and define boundaries by defining your relationship. Have convictions (not opinions) and make sure you don't jump into conclusions, misconceptions and infatuation.

THE KIND OF A WOMAN A MAN WANTS:

Everyman desires a woman who has Christ-like character, who is loyal, respectful, hospitable, nice, friendly and accommodating.

Also, every man seeks for a woman who is spiritual; who can stand in the gap for him in prayers when he is at work.

THE KIND OF A MAN A WOMAN WANTS:

Every woman desires a man who is willing to learn and adapt, one who is warm and forgiving, a man who puts the family's needs ahead of his, a man who is submissive, patient and forbearing; not bossy, a man who is mature enough to care for another, someone who doesn't have emotional baggage, a man with a steady job or a good business, a man who is from a reasonably good family, a man who is humble and patient with her weaknesses and willing to sacrifice his life for hers.

RIGHT CHOICE IN MARRIAGE

The bible tells us in the book of 2 Corinthians 6:14 that *"Be ye not unequally yoked together with unbelievers: for what fellowship hath righteousness with unrighteousness? and what communion hath light with darkness?"*. The Bible standard cannot be compromised and that is why we are encouraged to marry a Christian who has the fear of the Lord.

Apart from the choice of who to serve, choosing who to marry is another fundamental choice that affects the destiny of an individual. A wrong choice in marriage can negatively affect the choice to serve God. Solomon chose to marry many strange women and they influenced him to forsake God and serve their idols.

Solomon's earlier decision to serve the Almighty God was badly affected by his marriages. A marriage partner can take Heaven away from the dreams of his or her spouse and replace it with Hell. Depending on who you choose to marry, your relationship with God will either continue to improve or it will stop all together.

Solomon did not want to forget God who has done so much for him, but his marriage made him to err. It is vital to look at the factors that influence the choices we often make. There are always negative and positive factors guiding the choices we make. Whichever you allow to guide you will determine the kind of choice you will make.

Many people made costly mistakes in the Bible either because they ignorantly made a choice or because they relied entirely on their knowledge without recourse to God's guidance. Making a good choice therefore goes beyond human knowledge. No matter how much you know, depending on God in making a choice is a sign of meekness and humility. It is however unfortunate that many young folks today don't believe that God still chooses the right marriage partner for His obedient children. The Bible in Psalm 25:9 says: "The meek will he guide in judgment: and the meek will he teach his way." God guides the meek in judgment. Judgment in this context means decision, choice or preference.

You need basic knowledge in the areas where you have to make a choice. Nevertheless, after acquiring the requisite knowledge, you still need to depend on God. Lot chose a piece of land that he knew would be good for agriculture and he chose to relocate there. His knowledge was perfect, but it was limited because he did not know what the future held for that land. God later destroyed that land in the overthrow of Sodom and Gomorrah (Genesis 13:9-12).

There is nothing wrong in making a choice, but Lot's mistake was that he did not seek God's guidance in making his choice. Relying solely on what you know in making a choice can cost you your whole life and mar your eternal peace. As a youth, do you know enough about marriage before you dabble into it? Do not choose by sight; having the relevant knowledge and God's guidance are key to making the best choice.

THE THREE PEOPLE WHO CAN GUIDE YOU IN CHOOSEN

GOD – He is the one who created you and knows the best choice for you. The best choice comes from him and it is best to wait upon the Lord for marriage.

In the book of Genesis 24 and Genesis 28, we have examples of parents choosing for their children. Abraham made his chief servant promise that he'd find a good wife for his son, Isaac. And In Bedrock 28 of the same book, Jacob's parents choose for him, but his brother chose a wife for himself. God will lead you through his Holy Spirit. For this to happen, you need to be submissive.

OUR PARENTS- Your parents can decide your suitor, but if you have parents who are not believers in God, you can imagine the kind of husband they would prefer you have. In a family where the father is an idol worshipper, if he were to choose for his daughters, he would prefer to place his children in the hands of idol worshippers or chief priest.

YOURSELF – You can choose for yourself. However, this is when God has given you his own choice yet you decide he/she is not the one you love. At the end of the day, you marry that person of your choice, and it becomes a manage affair like Samson, Judges 14:1-5
May God help us all.

Can we hear from God?

There are people who hear from God, but when it comes to marriage, they are confused hoping that God will use another method, they never hear from him. Why? The same method God speaks to you for other things are the same way He will speak to you concerning marriage.

God can speak through an audible voice; however this is far and in-between. There are only few people who have this privilege from God. He can speak through dreams.

However, we need to be careful about dreams, because even the devil also confuses people, especially when they open their emotions to X-rated materials.

A man came to me one day and said, 'Pastor, I always have sex in my dream.' I asked him what he has been reading. Anyone who spends the night reading X-rated materials has opened himself to devil's wiles. The book of Ecclesiastes 5:3 tells us that: *For a dream cometh through the multitude of business; and a fool's voice is known by multitude of words.*

God can also speak through the bible. I remember a lady I was trusting God for to be my wife. As I lay to sleep, I dreamt; I saw a man like pastor who said God would speak to me in the morning through a bible verse. At that time I used to read '*Everyday with Jesus',* and the place I opened to read that day said, 'when you get to that land, do not marry.' At once I knew he had spoken to me concerning the lady.

God will speak to you in the way he has always spoken to you. May he speak to all of us in Jesus name.

WHY SHOULD WE MARRY?

We marry for the propagation of human race. Gen 9:1, for companionship and to avoid sin and to obey the commandment of God. Gen 1:28.

We also marry to have fellowship. Gen 2:18, for Partnership (one flesh) Gen 2:4 and to satisfy some holy and legitimate desires.

RELATIONSHIP THOUGHTS FOR ALL SINGLE MEN

1. Before you start a relationship with a lady, you must think carefully about what you are about to do. A relationship is not something you should rush into or handle lightly.

2. Are you ready for a relationship with her? Are you emotionally, mentally, financially and spiritually mature to meet her needs?

3. Being sexually attracted to her means absolutely nothing. It isn't a sign of likeness, love or any other thing your mind may come up with. It may just be your hormones messing with your mind. A woman is more than her body and her sexuality. She has a life which you should be able to blend with. Can you do that?

4. This lady has a history. Can you handle it? She has a past. Can you handle it? Can you handle her mistakes, failures and weaknesses? Can you handle her dreams without being intimidated and becoming jealous?

5. She already had a life before she met you. Can you fit into it and help improve her life?

6. Love is a commitment. Are you ready to commit your life to helping her grow and become all that she can be, by God's grace?

7. Is she valuable enough for you to devote a large portion of your life towards the accomplishment of her dream? Are you ready to pour your resources into making her all the

Lord plans for her to be? If you are not ready, don't just bother.

8. Before you open your mouth to say 'I love you', ask yourself if this is not just a moment of 'emotional madness'. A lady needs much more than 'I love you'. She needs your commitment. If you are not ready to make that commitment that will lead to marriage, please leave her alone in peace and stop wasting her time and resources.

LONELINESS

Loneliness could be a sign that you need somebody to marry. In Genesis 2:18, God said, *'It is not good for man to be alone...'* Adam was enjoying a great relationship with God, but because he didn't have a human companion, God said it wasn't a good thing.

God designed you with two voids. One is a void only he himself can fill. The other is a void only the right people can fill. The question then is: ***'What should I do?'*** Seek the face of God

WHEN SHOULD A CHRISTIAN MARRY?

A Christian Should marry when you have a good job, at least moderate accommodation with essential things, when you are mature to handle family challenges, when you have attained the age of maturity (Adulthood), when such Christian is led by God and not by emotion and ultimately when you are financially stable (at least able to feed yourself and wife.

Dating or courtship

Dating is the activity of going out on a date; the activity of going out regularly with somebody as a social or romantic partner.

Many Christian are confused about dating and courtship. There is nothing called dating in Christendom, it is a western culture and a sinful life. Courtship begins after both parties have reached a consensus, and the Pastor confirms their conviction and prays for them to start their courtship.

The first step into marriage is to know each other better. During this time, there must never be any sexual relationship between the two. Keep a holy distance as you avoid petting and caressing and above all keep yourself pure and holy.

Dating was invented in the early part of this century. Prior to that time, marriage always involved much more input from the parents, and "trial relationships" leading to marriage which may not be conducted at all.

"Dating" means different things to different people, particularly across generations. We can define "dating" as two people in an intimate relationship. The relationship may be sexual, but it does not have to be. It may be serious or casual, short-term or long-term. The important thing to remember is that dating abuse can occur within all kinds of intimate relationships.

Dating as a social relationship means going out together, being with someone or seeing each other as just friends Regardless of the label you use, you and your partner should both accept the same definition for your relationship.

Who is a dating partner?

Simply put, a dating "partner" refers to the person you're in a relationship with. A healthy partner is trustworthy, honest, dependable, and supportive.

Infatuation is lust not love

Let us consider the following scenario. Jessica and Darmian like each other. They met a few weeks ago at a dance and kissed. They want to get to know each other but don't know what to do next. Is this love or infatuation

CAN I DATE A MARRIED MAN?

As a single lady, you are not expected to get involved with a married man because this will lead to heartbreak. Here are some reasons as to why you shouldn't be dating a married man:

1. It is wrong: No matter how much you try to prove yourself right – there are no justifications when it comes to dating a married person. It is considered to be 'ethically wrong' and could hamper your life in more ways than one.

2. Second best: When you get involved with a married man, no matter how much he claims that you are his true love, at the end of the day, his wife and family (kids) will be his first priority. Remember that he will come up with a host of excuses to cover up for cheating on his family – but when it comes to choosing between his family and you, it will always be his family and not you.

3. Lies: Another reason not to get involved with a married man is lies. Men, who have a wife and children at home, will lie to you endlessly for not being able to meet up with you, or not being able to accompany you for shopping or a movie.

WHAT IS COURTSHIP?

Courtship: This is a prelude t*o marriage; that is* the period of a romantic relationship before marriage. This is a time when you try to gain somebody's love; when you pay attention to somebody with a view to developing a more intimate relationship.

It is one thing to choose the right partner in marriage; it is another thing to choose the right approach to courtship. A wrong approach to courtship, particularly Christian courtship, can have a negative impact on the right choice. Therefore, believers that are in courtship must be Christian through and through if they would eat the good of the land of marriage (Isaiah 1:19).

The important lesson for ladies to learn is that, a man is at his best in courtship. He would call you by different pet names. He would tease you and make you feel secure. These are the normal sweet words you would hear in courtship. However, when the wedding ceremony is over, his hidden shortcomings will be exposed because he can no longer hide them. The saying that "love is blind" is true but marriage is the tool to open the eyes of the blind lover. You will discover the real personality of a man or woman after the wedding ceremony.

For courtship to be Christian in nature, the admonition in God's word which is in the Bible must be our watchword. Courtship between two children of God must not be handled childishly. It should be handled with maturity as expected of a serious relationship. There are many false doctrines flying around and children of God must be aware of them. For example, some people believe that once you are in courtship, you can begin to co-habit, doing all sorts of ungodly things together. They call it "trial marriage". This has no place in Christianity. It is whore-mongering. More often than not, after these so-called brothers have had their fill of the so-called sisters, they dump the sisters for those they regard as "reserved and self-disciplined".

In the same vein, there are terrible wolves in sheep's clothing among some so-called sisters too. They try to make unsuspecting naïve brothers get them pregnant and the result is what we call shot-gun marriage. This is a marriage not properly prepared for.

Christian courtship must be characterised with sincere gestures. It involves sharing past and present experiences with your would-be wife or husband. It should look beyond the present to future aspirations. You should lay your future bare in the hands of Jesus Christ. Though there may be sincere disagreements during courtship, these are not strong enough reasons to break the courtship. However, if a courtship is full of troubles that you are almost getting suffocated with sinful or legalistic demands of your partner, you need to have a rethink. This situation calls for fresh prayer. You may have made a mistake in the first place.

Today, we are living in a highly corrupt and immoral world that even our culture teaches our singles to engage in ungodly way but we have to lay a good and solid foundation if we don’t want regrets in future.

As Christians, our primary purpose in life is to seek and serve God, and to fulfil our destiny in Him. This is equally true in the area of relationships. I want to call this ‘standard courtship’.

Courtship is about open and honest exploration of each other’s lives and families leading up to engagement and marriage. Courtship is about marriage – you court in order to see if there is any reason why you shouldn't get married. There is no romantic interaction until after the commitment to marriage.

Courtship is a word that has been adopted to describe a biblical model for the relationship leading up to marriage. In the Bible, the parents were always involved in the marriage process. They did not arrange the marriage without the children's consent, although they were certainly involved in the arrangement.

Marriage

When a man dates his wife-to-be, praise becomes an important part of courting. When he appreciates the beauty of her hair, he should express it to her verbally. He should complement her beauty, her choice of perfume and clothing, and her excellent taste. If he enjoys her cooking or a special gift, he should freely express his appreciation. If he admires the way she expresses herself, again, he should say something.

When you love someone, praise should come naturally because it's a genuine, stimulating part of a growing relationship. You should cultivate the habit of saying nice things to your spouse, accept her character, be humorous, compassionate, be generous and a hardworking man.

A man who ensures equality in his relationship will enjoy the best of his woman. Every lady wants a man with a moving vision, not the one that claim what is not, but with humility disclose his statures and ready to grow. Everybody needs compassion but the woman needs it more. Every lady will like a man that appreciates team work and a neat guy. Every lady wants a friend not a boss.

THE DOS AND DON'TS IN COURTSHIP

Courtship is the gap between saying yes and when you say I do. Courtship begins immediately your parents and spiritual leaders have agreed with your proposal. It is a period of sober reflection; a time to build spiritual family foundation, a time to know some mystery about whom you are about to marry, a time to plan for your future and it is also a time to apply the principle of '**HAB'.** Help him to change, Adapt to his life style or Break the relationship

Courtship is not the time to test how good you can cook, watch movies, have sex, or help each other. Don't ever sleep together. It is not a time for kissing, romance or cohabiting.

Things That Weaken Relationships

They include criticism, complaints, coercion, confrontation, lies, broken promise, and ultimately lack of communication.

Also a dangerous killer of relationships is the competitive urge where those in relationships are always looking for an advantage, the upper hand, some edge they can hold over their partner's head.

Competitive spirit is the cause of many relationships that aren't working presently. Sometimes this issue of competition can be very subtle and indirect in the way it affects relationships. Innocently, we may think it's all about trying to challenge one another to do more, give more, perform more and sacrifice more. Truly, it's not bad to have such motive. But something is wrong whenever we turn our relationship to a competition where one partner must play to win and outrun the other partner.

Please always remember this: You are never in a relationship for Win-Lose game. You are not in a relationship to show you can do what your partner cannot do, and you think that makes you better than the person. You are not in a relationship to compete but to complete the other person.

The best relationships have been ruined by competition, leaving one of the partners devastated, incapable and broken-down. But instead of trying to outdo, outrun or outperform your partner – it is more profitable to 'co-do',' co-run', and 'co-perform' with your partner. Seek for ways you can win together. Don't be a champion of your relationship and make your partner the victim of defeat.

Coercion: Every relationship that engages in competition will produce two different types of people – a winner or a loser. And often than not, the so called "loser" becomes a lawful slave to the "winner" and the result is a relationship where coercion is the language in what they do and how they do it.

Coercion is simply a concept of using the pressure approach and the enforcement approach to achieve your desires – whether good or bad in your relationship. The other partner who is under-performing or not bringing so much into the relationship will be automatically put under pressure, intimidation, compulsion and the dictatorship of the winner.

Competition drives coercive spirit in a relationship, and finally ruins it. Any relationship where one of the partners feels to be under pressure of the other partner is no longer a relationship. It has become a slave-master bond.

But we must always remember that God has not given us a relationship where partners must mount pressure and make life unbearable for the other.

Confrontation is another dangerous killer of relationships. It is not bad in itself, but it can be dangerous if it is not properly done. It is not bad if you are dissatisfied about something in your partner and you want it changed, improved or corrected.

It is bad only when you do it wrongly; keeping scores of wrong, using position of authority, disrespectfully, discourteously, impolitely, indecorously and with wrong motive.

But confrontation is healthy when you pray before you make the move, follow the prompting and leading of the Holy Spirit, speak the truth in love, care about the other person, deal with the matter wisely, and be ready to listen, encourage positive response in the other person and work towards a lasting resolution.

I pray the Lord will give you the Grace to manage your relationship wisely in Jesus name.

Things that will improve a relationship

You must show genuine enthusiasm when you are greeting your partner. Show him or her respect and be supportive. Give your wife be a benefit of doubt and let her know you appreciate her. Give her the chance to contribute to your life while allowing him or her to know more about you. When you show your partner good attitude, you respect him/her by forgiving his/her mistakes; you will have a perfect relationship.

Many marriages are in crisis today because many married people have deviated from what God intended marriage to be. What you see today are marriages as men want it and not as God intended it.

When you compare your wife with your ex- girlfriend is a sign that you have not left your past. Don't ever discuss private things that happen in your marriage with your family members which may ultimately create a negative impression of him/her.

Friends, it is high time we tell ourselves the unclad truth. If you want to enjoy being married, be responsible. There is a lot of responsibility that God placed on men. Let us see what God expects of husbands in the Bible:

"... love your wife, just as Christ loved the Church and gave Himself for it" Ephesians 5:25

If you appreciate how much Christ loved the Church and gave Himself for it, you will know the magnitude of being responsible as a husband and father. An irresponsible husband is likely to be an irresponsible father and you know Christ is not like that.

The Bible also says:

"...love your wife as your own body. He who loves his wife loves himself" Ephesians 5:28

It is in your own interest to love your wife. If you love her; you love yourself.

"...dwell with them with understanding, giving honour to the wife as to the weaker vessel, and as being heirs together of the grace of life, that your prayers may not be hindered" I Peter 3:7

Simply put, you hinder yourself by the way you treat your wife. If it is true that man was created in the image and likeness of God, it is time we wake up to the expectation of our Maker.

How Long Should Courtship be?

Rushing to the altar isn't such a smart move. Experts agree that you should wait at least a year. It can take a good six months or so to remove the love-coloured glasses and begin to really see the other person's flaws. That's because the longer you steadily date, the more you get out of your comfort zones and settle into a routine—and that's when your true personalities emerge. Is he lazy about doing household chores? Is he disrespectful to your family and friends?

Before you can determine if your love will go the distance, you need enough time to go by to make sure you have similar outlooks on handling money, whether you want kids, and other crucial thoughts about the future. To sustain a relationship, couples have to share common goals, values, and interests along with sexual attraction and emotional maturity.

During courtship, you are not supposed to demand for sex, use insulting words on your would be partner, check the cell phone or email of your partner without permission. Watch out for extreme jealousy or insecurity, explosive temper and whether he/she has a mood swings.

Don't Rush into This Relationship after any disappointment

When we feel hurt and rejected there's something inside us that wants to prove we're still worthy and desirable. As a result we can jump into the next relationship too quickly. But just like an infant doesn't go from crawling to driving overnight, there is a process involved, and if you try to circumvent it you will end up in square one.

A new relationship won't successfully heal you, avoid aggravating inflicted wounds, or instantly clean up a mess…regardless of the temporary bliss, sooner or later you'll end up faced again with the same situation.

'Solomon writes, *don't excite love, don't stir it up, until the time is ripe- and you're ready*. 'Don't be in such a hurry to take the edge off your pain that you run ahead of God. It takes time for Him to make you into the person He wants you to become. While He's working on you, He is preparing the heart of the right partner to show up at the right time. In the meantime, there is a way to fill the emptiness inside, when you develop a closer relationship with God.
We all want to be loved and appreciated for who we are; and when it doesn't happen on our timetable, we make everything better. Marriage would be better if the husband and the wife clearly understand that they are on the same side.

True love is not having premarital and extramarital sexual escapades; it is about loving God deeply, loving people genuinely, contributing to the lives of others and obeying the principles of holiness that are clearly taught in the Holy Scriptures.

Love is all about sacrifice, patience, giving, and commitment. Whether the person has done very well or badly, you still love him or her. That kind of love Jesus has for the church, while we were yet sinners Christ died for us.

Lust is when you want to get a particular thing from someone and after you have gotten it, you don't really love that individual anymore. Lust is what is common most especially in teenagers of today.

The dictionary definition of lust is the Intense or unrestrained sexual craving, or an overwhelming desire or craving."

In Matthew 5:28, the bible recorded that "But I say, anyone who even looks at a woman with lust in his eye has already committed adultery with her in his heart." Also, Job 31:11-12 (NLT) sums up lust quite nicely: *"For lust is a shameful sin, a crime that should be punished. It is a devastating fire that destroys to hell. It would wipe out everything I own."*

Don't ever fail to pray before saying yes to a man. Don't be in a hurry to get married. If you rush in, you may rush out with a lot of injuries. Discover your purpose before marriage. As a man or woman, add value to yourself and live a good life.

As a sister, don't run after a man because of his money, cars connection, position, talent, or family background; marry a man based on the conviction of the Holy Spirit and love. Develop a healthy eating habit and don't be too fat that single men begin to think you are married.

Dress well. First impression counts. Don't expose any of your private part for men to see otherwise you might only attract a player not a responsible man. Don't beg or force a man to marry you; you are too precious to do that. Your character is your marriage; so work on your character. Beauty is not everything; if it is all you have, you'll lose your place to someone more beautiful and more matured than you.

Never fail to learn how to cook good food. Men usually love a woman who feed them with good food because one of the easiest ways to a man's heart is through good food and above all, never fail to give your life to Christ before marriage. A marriage without Christ is bound to experience marital crisis.

Maturity is essential in marriage.

There is a depth of maturity regarding marriage. Before Eve came, Adam was already a man and not a boy. Marriage is for a fully-grown and matured man and not for boys. It is also for a fully-grown and matured woman not for girls. The partner must be filled with the breath of God. The Man must be alive and filled with the breath of God to be able to successfully marry (Genesis 2:7).

Adam received the breath of God and became a living soul. The man must be a living man which means that he must be born-again. Lots of relationships outside of Christianity are based on the wrong foundation and are not really working the way it should. If a man/woman is not truly born again or understand the things of God, they cannot truly understand or appreciate marriage.

Resources needed to sustain the relationship must be in place.

Adam was already in the Garden of Eden before Eve joined him. Everything you need to sustain a relationship must be available within the relationship and not far from it. A relationship should not be expensive or costly. There is bound to be conflict if a relationship is too expensive, or if you have to go far outside of it to get things to sustain the relationship. You must be able to operate within your limits. Please avoid "high maintenance" relationship, except you are very rich. A lot of marriages or relationships are based on financial considerations.

For some women the more money spent; the deeper the love. This is not necessarily so; I pray however, you will not marry a miser. Men should learn to be generous to their wives with what they have. Women should also look out for a man who has the following in place before they gets married:

- **A Home:** A man must have his own place. It could be just a room or even a small flat but it should be his or one on which he is the one paying the rent. A serious relationship needs a home that the man is responsible for. Living with ones parents can be very stressful.

- **A Job**: Adam had a job. A man must be doing something productive for God and humanity, and have a purpose and a vision. Be under God's instruction: Genesis 2:16 says, *"The Lord commanded."* You must be under the instruction of God to be able to successfully manage your marriage. Be ready to listen to God. Adam and Eve's disobedience of God's instruction, led to the first marital breakdown, quarrel, loss of face and dignity. The devil will always test the relationship so we all need to be watchful.
  Have ample knowledge of how to survive in life: A man should have received the instructions for survival. The Lord told Adam not to eat of a certain tree. It means that every man needs to know what he needs to do to survive

in life. A man who cannot survive cannot successfully manage a marriage.

- **Have a vision**: The man should have a vision. Do not get involved with a man who does not know where he is going or is unable to tell you where he is going or a woman who does not know what she wants.

  In any relationship you must be ready to see the faults, accept them, make excuses for them and move on. Learn to love and love deeply. How many of us are ready to be there always; in good or bad, rough or easy, tough or smooth conditions, how many? How many are living with imagination rather than dealing with reality?

  A relationship is not for sex. It is much more than that. A relationship is for the completion of an established man or woman. You see, marriage is a covenant till death. What they say is "till death do us part." If it is so dangerous then a decision concerning it should not be taken lightly. It is my prayer that the Lord will make us of quick understanding and enable us to do the right thing and do things right.

Before you say I do

Before you say I do, find out about the genotype of your partner. For instance if you are AA and the lady is AA, you are on the right path. If you are AA and your partner is AS; this still okay. If you are AA and your partner is SS; you may still get married but if the man is AS and the woman is AS too; you have to increase your faith and in a situation you are AS and your partner is SS; know that there is fire on the mountain and if the two of you are both SS, don't try it because the children that may come from such relationship will give you stress all the days of your life.

Let us look consider the story of Uriah and Bathsheba: the union between Uriah and Bathsheba was no exception because they had their own problems.
How do I know that Uriah and Bathsheba had their problems? The first reason is that Bathsheba fell easily for another man to have an affair with her. The second reason is the fact that Uriah was reluctant to go home. Why was the marriage of Uriah and Bathsheba not working?

Uriah marriage was against the will of God.
Uriah was a Hittite while Bathsheba was a Jew. God had told the Jews specifically not to marry the Canaanites Deuteronomy 7:1-4. If you marry against God's will then you are bound to have problems

They were from different backgrounds. Bathsheba was a princess in Israel while Uriah was a Hittite. You may be spiritually compatible but you may have different backgrounds; different families, different friends and different attitudes to life. We need to understand who we really are and what our backgrounds are.

They had different visions. Uriah had a vision to serve the King and his Country but Bathsheba was a woman in love with her own body and in displaying her assets. A lot of couples live completely separate lives. There are also changing attitudes and changing circumstances in a marriage which some couples do not address.

They did not have any Children. Childlessness can be a source of stress in a marriage.

Their sex life was poor. There is no where it is written that Uriah went to sleep with his wife. Sex can be a problem whether it is too much or too little.

Lack of understanding of what marriage is all about. A lot of people go into marriages with storybook ideas. We need to understand the whole concept of marriage.

Bedrock 3: HOW TO MANAGE YOUR MARRIAGE

For any good thing to last you need to manage them. E.g. Car, house, machine, marriage even life; our major challenge is that we lack maintenance culture. Communication is very important in any relationship. Don't use sex as a weapon against your partner. This may cause unexplainable quarrel.

Food, your appearances, job, In-laws, friends and time may be another cause of quarrel in marriage. As you manage it well may God help you to sustain your marriage for life in Jesus name.

Don't go to bed without doing this:

Resolve every matter, forgive them and yourself, plan for tomorrow, read scripture even if it is one line in the Holy book, make yourself happy and give your life to Jesus

Most people get married believing a myth that marriage is a box full of all the things they have longed for: companionship, intimacy, friendship etc. The truth is that marriage at the start is an empty box. You put something in before you can take anything out. There is no love in marriage. Love is in people and people put love in marriage. There is no romance in marriage; you have to infuse it into your marriage.

A lot of people especially ladies look forward to marriage and think that once they marry all their problems would be solved. Statistics has it that a lot of marriages have problems.

As a matter of fact, in America, the divorce rate is about 55%. A lot of other couples are living like strangers, sleeping in different rooms, following very different routines. Some couples go for as long as 9 months without any sexual interaction, some don't even talk for weeks. A lot of people suddenly marry and find out that they have nothing in common, many a couple have regretted the day of their marriage and many are having extra marital affairs.

A lot of marriages have major problems and what you find a lot of times are couples just managing to live together in mutual tolerance.

Anyone who has mastered that profound fact that love is reciprocal, and is willing to dedicate himself, without reservation or demand for return, to the needs and fulfilment of others, will certainly be loved and be fulfilled within him.

Basically, if you want to find love, you've got to give love. Love is often difficult to practice in our society today where deep relationships are hard to establish, and as such there's more of a pull towards easy, impersonal and less committing contacts.

A passion for unity

"...with longsuffering, forbearing one another in love; endeavoring to keep the unity of the spirit" Ephesians4:2-3.
If unity was a wall, each of us would be a brick, no two of us would occupy the same slot and all of us would be held together by the mortal of "longsuffering". The word longsuffering means "to remain calm, to stay together in every circumstance and to have a focus that transcends our present discomfort". Think about that!

Without a passion for unity, we'll never have it, for there is a cost attached. It involves yielding to one another preferring one another Rom.12:10, preserving regardless of the difficulties Gal. 6:9, protecting our unity, because ultimately it's the source of our blessing Eph.4:19.

"Behold, how good and how pleasant it is for brethren to dwell together in unity! It is like the precious ointment upon the head that ran down upon the beard, even Aaron's beard: that went down to the skirts of his garments...For there the Lord commanded the blessing" Ps. 133:1-3.

There is two-way method of creating a stronger bond in your relationship; which is compassion. Compassion is the desire to ease others' suffering by taking their burdens away from them. It is a sympathetic awareness of another' distress combined with a desire to alleviate it.
It is simply kindness and caring in action.

Compassion helps us make positive difference in people's lives. It creates a bond that glues the hearts of people in a relationship together. Whenever compassion is shown to another person, we are simply demonstrating our love.

In life you can never be too kind or too fair; everyone you meet is carrying a heavy load. When you go through your day expressing kindness and courtesy to all you meet, you leave behind a feeling of warmth and good cheer, and you help alleviate the burdens everyone is struggling with." It is not possible to say you love someone and remain indifferent, uncaring, insensible, inattentive, callous, and hard-hearted to their needs.

Compassionate relationship is always others oriented; it seeks to make others happy. It creates mutual benefits for the person showing it and the one receiving it. Such that, when we feel love and kindness toward others, it not only makes others feel loved and cared for, but it helps us also to develop inner happiness and peace.

There is a sense of personal fulfilment that we enjoy through compassionate living that nothing else gives.
We need to develop ourselves in this strong quality of relationship bonding through the power of the Holy Spirit. It will really bring the best out of our relationships. I pray the Lord will grant us the Grace in Jesus name.

On the wedding day, the man is called the bridegroom. There's a reason for that. Take that word-apart and it becomes pretty obvious: He's meant to be the BRIDE-GROOM. That's not just a ceremonial designation. It's actually a job description. The job of the husband is to 'groom' his wife. It subtly connotes an agricultural activity: to tend, to care for, to help improve, to supply essentials for growth and to bring out the best. The husband is not meant to be the 'bride-groom' on just the wedding day (and night); that's what he should be for the rest of his life. He should never stop tending, developing and inspiring his bride to the fullness of her potentials.

So young man, before you open your mouth to start 'delivering your manifesto', take a good look at your toolbox and ask yourself "Is my 'grooming kit complete?" "What exactly do I have to offer beyond things?" "Am I prepared to 'groom' this 'vine' or am I just craving for its fruits?"

And dear young lady, before you get carried away with whatever you're seeing, ask yourself: "does he have what it takes to help me become a better person?" It's not just about if he can give you better things. What's his effect on your person thus far? Are you becoming a better woman because of your association with him? Is there more clarity in your life? More discipline, more kindness, a better walk with God, More inner beauty.

Therefore, belonging to the same, spiritual kingdom; in the realm of the soul, both of them should have the same mind concerning various matters, especially the principles of the doctrine of Christ as stated in Heb.6:1-2, for two cannot walk except they agree Amos 3:3. In the realm of the body, both must accept the fact that their bodies belong to each other and must be ready to share it with one another.

Scripturally, this union is for a life time. It should therefore, not to be entered into unadvisedly. It is important to know what marriage is all about before one says "I do" to anyone. Marriage is not peculiar to any culture or country of the world. It is heaven's culture. It is therefore not traditionalist in any way, but scriptural. God's word gives us guidance on what needs to be known about it in order to make it successful.

Since Marriage was instituted by God Himself, anyone who wants success in marriage should make God the centre of such a relationship. God is the only sure foundation for success in marriage.

DWELING TOGETHER IN UNITY

In the book of Psalm 133:1-3, the Bible records the following account; "Behold how good and how pleasant it is for brethren to dwell together in unity". Facts on the ground keep showing that much of the societal ills prevalent in our days stem from men, women, boys and girls who have been raised from broken homes. There are some of such homes which are not broken so to say, but the man and the woman in there are best described as strangers dwelling together.

It is worrisome, to say the least, what activities go on amongst teenagers who are from these homes. It appears many families are helping to destroy the lives of these children and the future of our society by the careless way they handled the matter of marriage.

If the church must not fail in its "traditional" role of being a light to the world and salt to the earth, we must at this point sit down and examine this disturbing trend. As we do this we must allow the word of God to guide us so that lives can be salvaged again, our society can be better, and the world can become a better place to live in.

It is not enough to just dwell together, doing so in bond of love; unity, is very important. Unity is more than a physical affair; it must first start from the heart.

THE SECRET OF A SUCCESSFUL MARRIAGE

For a marriage to be successful, the couple must embrace love instead of like. Some religious leaders have at different times said that understanding is greater than love. God is love and love is a spirit. One could love through an unending performance.

To make your marriage work, endeavour to understand your spouse by adjusting and identifying the weak points of your spouse. Your tolerance is extremely important.

Adjustment is necessary in every marriage relationship. You need to recognize that there will always be ups and downs and this is quite normal. You only need to adjust to the dynamic nature of the relationship. Flexibility is good because we know that change is the only constant thing in life. So, once the change is beneficial to both parties and they both agree to it, just go for it, it makes the marriage vibrant and alive.

Christ as the divine head in every family and this is followed by the Husband the human head of the family, the Wife and the children who are the heritage of the Lord.

Forgiveness is very important in any relationship because no couple is perfect and you cannot rule out disagreement in your relationships. It is called Marriage Dispute.

Recognize that your marriage deserves the best in nature and care. In return it would grow strong and not fail. Everything that has breath needs love, care and good nurturing. A baby that is well cared for, loved, nurtured will thrive, so will a marriage. So put effort into making your marriage thrive well.

Note that from the time the marriage vows were made, you became one with your spouse and that union is bigger than any individual and as such every action or decision taken should be for the good of the two people rather than one individual. Let your spouse needs be paramount to yours.

Giving is an important part of having a filled marriage. When you give it will be given back to you, pressed down, shaken together and running over.

Sometimes one partner is so pre-occupied with receiving that the art of giving is forgotten. This is not fair, but it is also selfish. The one who keeps giving and does not receive will feel forgotten soon.

When you don't give, it shows that you do not love. Giving does not have to be just gifts, even though gifts are good and important but giving could be in terms of time, attention, support, empathy, consideration, self, forgiveness and understanding.

Communication is about the most important aspect of marriage. You cannot have a fulfilled marriage except you are communicating. You need to let your spouse know your thoughts, feelings, needs and expectations. Don't keep any information from each other.

Communication is a skill that you have to work on. It is the pipe that feeds the marriage. Once it is starved, the marriage stops thriving and it slowly dies. As you practice communication with your spouse it will get better and better until you find out that your spouse knows your feeling, needs, want, expectations and fears.

Spend Quality Time Together. There is nothing that can replace quality time spent together. Relationships are built on shared experiences and experience requires time. When you do things together in love, it is far better than any gift or favour you can get or give to him/her.

Focus on Christ. Once you have given your lives to Christ, you must hand the relationship over to Him as well. Your marriage should be centered on Christ. God is love and if you want love in your marriage then you must invite Jesus Christ into your home.

The sexual relationship cannot be separated from the rest of the relationship. Instead a strong exiting sexual relationship serves as a measure of the total relationship. It is wrong to withhold sex from one another. It is a non-verbal way of punishing each other or expressing anger and it's unhealthy. Of course you need to keep the lines of communication open so that the sexual bond between both of you can wax stronger as the years go by.

Recognize that your marriage deserves the best in nature and care. In return it would grow strong and not fail. Everything that has breath needs love, care and good nurturing. So put effort into making your marriage thrive well. From the time the marriage vows were made you became one with your spouse. That union is bigger than any individual and as such, every action or decision taken should be for the good of the two people rather than an individual.

Ensure to attend the same worship centre with your spouse. Do things in common and do not go contrary to the wish of your spouse.

Finally, there are three persons that make up a marriage which has been defined above while using mathematical term. This formulation represents a means of communication. For instance, in the Garden of Eden (which was the most beautiful and well-planned city till eternity), the first couple lost this golden opportunity when they allowed the fourth person to come in into their marriage. Satan penetrated into their marriage through the serpent (if you recall, the first couple had no relatives, siblings, children, or friends). They had access to different animals that accompanied and played with them. So, Satan had no option than to bribe the serpent for him to penetrate into that beautiful union.

BENEFITS OF ATTENDING CHURCH AS A FAMILY

In today's fast-paced and frantic world, Sundays may be the only time that your family is able to catch up on much-needed rest and relaxation in preparation for another hectic week. Getting up early and making sure everyone is ready for service may seem more like work than an enjoyable way to end the weekend, but there are definite benefits to being actively involved in your church.

Finding the right church may require a bit of trial and error, but your happiness within a congregation is largely dependent upon your family's ability to fit in there and feel welcomed. Keep searching until you find a Church that brings you that peace, and attend it regularly.

ENVY IS TOO HEAVY DON'T CARRY IT
(A Joke)

A man was sick and tired of going to work every day while his wife stayed home. He wanted her to see what he went through so he prayed:

''Dear Lord; I go to work every day and put in 8 hours while my wife merely stays at home. I want her to know what I go through, so please allow her body to switch with mine for a day Amen``

God, in his infinite wisdom, granted the man's wish

The next morning, sure enough, the man awake as a woman:-

He arose, cooked breakfast for his mate and kids woke up the kids, set out for their School clothes, packed their lunches, drove them to school, come home and picked up dry cleaning, took it to the cleaners and stopped at the bank to make a deposit, went grocery shopping, then drove home to put away groceries, paid the bill and balance the check book. He cleaned the cat's litter box and bathed the dog. Then it

was already 1:00pm, he hurried to make the beds, do the laundry, empty dustbin, and sweep and mop the kitchen floor. Ran to school to pick up the kids and got into argument with them on the way home. Set out milk and cookies and got the kids organized to do their homework, then set up the ironing board and watched TV while he did the ironing.
At 4:30 he began peeling potatoes and washing vegetables for salad, receded the pork chops and snapped fresh beans for supper.
After supper, he cleaned the kitchen, ran the dishwasher, folded laundry, bathed the kids, and put them to bed.
At 9P.M he was exhausted and, though his daily chores weren't finished, he went to bed where he was expected to make love, which he managed to get through without complaint.
The next morning, he awake and immediately knelt by the bed and said "Lord, I don't know what I was thinking. I was so wrong to envy my wife's being able to stay home all day. Please, oh! Oh! Please, let us trade back."
The Lord, in his infinite wisdom, replied "my son, I feel you have learned your lesson and I will be happy to change things back to the way they were. You'll just have to wait nine months though. You got pregnant last night."

DUTIES OF THE HUSBAND AND THE WIFE

When it comes to relationships, there some personality traits men look for in a lifelong partner. The bible tells us in Matthew 2:14 *she is companion to her husband to talk together, to reason together and do things in common.* Show affection, be eager to please him. Don't only tell him how much you love but prove it in care and deeds.

Be free when you are with your husband. It is true that problems, concerns, and worries are part of life but don't let them affect your interaction with him. Try your best to enjoy your husband's company without letting him see that you are affected by life's cares.

Accepting and forgiving. You must love your husband no matter the circumstance; forgive him whenever he offends you. Support his vision, ministry so that he will succeed or be fulfilled. Pray for him always so that when the devil strikes, both of you will be able to withstand the wiles of the devil.

Be the woman your husband fell in love with from the start and keep that every day. Most women tend to change after they've gotten married in terms of how they take care of themselves and in their attitudes. Let your man see every day beauty of which you were when he fell in love with you.
Express your true beauty and let your husband see it all the time. Let your natural beauty (external and internal) shine out more than wearing makeup or trying to be someone you are not.

Put variety in your life. Avoid doing the same thing every day in every aspect of your personal expression and overall marriage life. Surprise your husband even through simple gestures such as wearing a different dress/blouse, wearing your hair a little bit differently or cooking something he hasn't tried before.

Take good care of your body and your fitness. Beautify and perfume yourself, put on nice and attractive clothes and bath regularly. After the monthly period, remove any blood traces or bad smells. Cleanliness and personal hygiene is paramount to healthy living and it should not be taken for granted.

Children should be taught from childhood to wash their teeth early in the morning. Fasting must not be an excuse. Having your bath in the morning and in the evening, if necessary, and dealing with body odour with body deodorant if you sweat a lot is not a sin. We must be pure within and without to stand in the presence of God. We must have clean hands and a pure heart. Abraham offered water to an angel to wash his feet as a sense of cleanliness.

For sisters; to improve your outlook and presentation, your hair must not be left uncared for so as to avoid stinking. When you look neat, you will not scare away sinners to whom we want to preach to. Generally, we are to be properly dressed with clean clothes all the time. Ps.24:3-4; Gen.18:4; 1Pt.3:3; Mk.14:3

Avoid your husband observing you in dirty clothes or rough shape. Avoid prohibited types of ornamentation, e.g. tattoo.

Use the types of perfumes, colours, and clothes that your husband likes. Change your hair styles, perfumes, etc. from time to time. However, among these things you should avoid excessiveness.

After returning from work, school, travel, or whatever has separated you, begin with a good greeting; meet him with a cheerful face, start with good news and delay any bad news until he has rested, receive him with loving and yearning sentences, make sure food is ready on time.

Majority of people in problem were women because they were ungrateful and deny the good done to them. The result of being grateful is that your husband will love you more and will do his best to please you in more ways. The result of being ungrateful is that your husband will be disappointed and will start asking himself: why should I do well to her, if she never appreciates? 1 Peter 3:5-6

Hasten for intercourse when your husband feels compulsion for it, make the first move. Don't always wait for him to initiate sex. Tease and tantalize him by exchanging loving phrases with your husband. Leave your husband to fully satisfy his desire, choose suitable times and good occasions for exciting intercourse, e.g. after returning from a travel, weekends, etc.

You shouldn't be depressed because your husband is poor or works in a simple job. You should look at the poor, sick, and handicapped people and remember
God for all He has given to you. You should remember that real wealth lies in giving, not getting and in contentment.

You should not consider this world as your hope and interest. You should not ask your husband for many unnecessary things. Asceticism does not mean not to enjoy what is good and permissible, but it means that one should look forward to the hereafter and
utilize whatever God has given. Encourage your husband to reduce expenses and save some money in order to give charity, feed the poor and the needy.

It is very common among ministers and workers in the church to be disorderly in public places and even in the church. This attitude shows lack of spiritual home training. For example, rushing for food or chairs in a large gathering, jumping queue in public places, flagrant disregard for decorum, driving against traffic, littering the environment with wastes, reckless talks, and lack of table manners and improper dressing of any kind. **2 Cor.3:2; Deut.22:5; 1 Cor.10:31; Phil.3:16-18.**

Your devotion and loyalty particularly in times of calamities is extremely important e.g. when he has an accident or bankrupt. You are expected to support him through your own work, money, and properties if needed.

Husband is the leader of the family, and the wife is his support and consultant. Eph. 5:33 and Eph. 5:22-24- She must be submissive, respective, honourable and reverence her husband in all manner of approach.

Please him if he is angry. Try to avoid what will bring his anger; but if it happens that you can't, then try to appease him. If you are mistaken, then apologize. If he is mistaken then, keep still instead of arguing or wait until he is no longer angry and discuss the matter peacefully with him. If he was angry because of external reasons then, keep silent until his anger goes. Find excuses for him, e.g. tired, problems at work, someone insulted him. Don't ask many questions and insist on knowing what happened, e.g. you should tell me what happened? I must know what made you so angry. You are hiding something, and I have the right to know.

Be conscious of saving/ spending. Save for the raining day. Put money away for things like vacations, home renovations, the kids. Protect yourself from any prohibited relationships. Keep the secrets of the family, particularly intercourse and things that the husband doesn't like other people to know. Take care of the house and children. Take care of his money and properties. Do not go out of your house without his permission. Refuse people whom he does not like to come over. Do not allow any man to be alone with you in any place. Be good to his parents and relatives in his absence.

You should welcome his guests and try to please them, especially his parents. You should avoid problems as much as you can with his relatives.

You should avoid putting him in a position where he had to choose between his mother and his wife. Show good hospitality to his guests by arranging a nice place for them to sit in. Welcome their wives, etc. Encourage him to visit his relatives and invite them to your home.

Phone his parents and sisters, send letters to them, buy gifts for them, support them in calamities, etc. Make your home better than his mother's home. Most men feel freedom at their mother's place where he grew up and was nurtured and after marriage you want to offer that kind of haven to him. Make your home warmer and more comfortable to him with lots of loving presence. Jealousy is a sign for wife's love for her husband but it should be kept within the limits.

Stay with him through thick and thin. Life is difficult and there will be challenges for everyone. It's important if a woman can support her man through the hard times, because there will be some. Be patient when you face poverty and strained circumstances.

Humility is one of the important etiquettes of Christian homes. Abraham and Lot, his nephew, learnt this from their parents. They bowed down to angels. This shows that they were humble even to strangers.

In the name of modernization, some parents do not raise their children to greet their elders or to humble themselves before them. Some, in the name of culture disrespect elders, forgetting that culture is the making of man while the Bible is the truth that must be followed by all cultures and races. Any child that lacks home training provides unnecessary negative exposure to his or her parents. If you are humble, there is nothing that you desire that you cannot have. Abraham got his promised child and Lot escaped the destruction of Sodom. Gen.18:2, 19:1; Mt.23:12; Jam.4:6, 10; 1Pt.5:6.

Cooperate with your husband and remind him of different obligatory and voluntary worships. Do not let small things get in the way of enjoying bonding time together with your husband such as irritation, smell, grudges, finances, etc. Support your husband in every aspect and show your love to him unconditionally without regrets. Encourage him to pray at night. Support your husband's activities by encouraging him, offering wise opinions, soothing his pains, etc. Prov. 12:4

Keep your home clean, decorated and well arranged. Change house arrangements from time to time to avoid boredom. Make a table of food and prepare healthy foods. Learn all the necessary skills for managing the house, e.g. sewing.
Learn how to raise children properly and in a Christian way.

Do not spend from his money, even for charity without his permission unless you are sure that he agrees on this. Protect his house, car, etc. while he is absent. Keep the children in good shape, clean clothes, etc. Take care of their nutrition, health, education, manners, etc. Teach them godly and moral behaviours and tell them the stories of the Bible and companions.

You are to teach them the Bible, principle of Godly living, teach them to love Christ and live like Him, teach them to identify with Christ, conforming to the ways of Christ in selflessness, love, patience and benevolence. For you to succeed, let the child see Jesus in you, this will make his/her conservation much easier. Also encourage Godliness in the child.

Don’t look for shortcomings, don't be suspicious, Be submissive, share interests, find humour/laugh together, his happiness is important, show that you care, comfort and appreciate him. Help him overcome obstacles.

Don’t get complacent, ask for his opinion, maintain yourself, buy something just for him, take care of your appearance, Support your husband, Be a woman of Prayer, Be trustworthy, Be positive minded, forgive him and respect him, be wise in dealing with your in-laws.

“Train up a child in the way he should go: and when he is old, he will not depart from it.” Proverbs 22:6. In the present day society and even in Christian families, parents have neglected home lessons in the name of modernization. Some ethical and moral behaviours of the bible have been relegated to the background. It is high time we took a cue from the bible to re-order the voice of the so-called modernization. Looking at humility, cleanliness and hospitality as virtues of good Christian homes where there is good home training.

Today, we will be looking into other moral and ethical behaviours expected from a child that has good home training. She must know that she will give account of her home most especially her children. She needs to train them in the ways of God so that they will be useful to the glory of God their maker. Prov. 22:6. She needs to lead them right and those who are leaving with them.

Hospitality is part of home training lessons that parent should give their children. Children should be taught the evil of stinginess and blessing of generosity in Christian’s homes and the Church of God. Some ministers of God do not really know that hospitality is an important duty in the ministry. Abraham, Lot and David were good examples of hospitable people in the Bible.

If you are stingy, the cup of water you cannot give can rob you of precious and very costly blessings. You could entertain angels without knowing. Heb.13:1-3; Mk.9:41; Lk.6:38; Gen.18:5-10; Prov.11:24; 1Kings.17:11-14; 2Kgs.4:8-17.

Women needs at least 30 minutes of uninterrupted time with their husbands each day. Twenty-four percent of women who claim to be in unhappy relationships spend fewer than five minutes a day with their spouses.
Ask yourself, "How much time do I spend with my spouse?" Uninterrupted time means time spent without iPhones and BlackBerry

Nowadays, women take care of the children and make salaries, and they tend to be much underappreciated. Women should be expressive of what makes them feel appreciated, saying, "These are the kinds of things I like … x, y and z." Men should listen, and women should also tune in when their husbands are appreciative.

It's important for women to have men who understand them. It's also important for women to help men understand how to listen. Men often don't have a clue, they are not good listeners. Women have to be sensitive of a time limit to their conversation.

More often than not, men are sitting there thinking, "When is this going to end?" I would say 15 to 20 minutes, max. Women should say to their husbands, "It's 8:00 p.m.; I need you to listen until 8:20 p.m." Women may deserve 10 hours, but most men are not the best at listening to serious, emotional conversations that goes on.

Fun is one of those things that often go out the window, especially after the first child is born. All the factors like jobs, rents or mortgages can add to relationship strain. Couples should set up a date night — once every week, even if they are tired — during which they spend a minimum of two hours alone. During this time, the couple should talk about everything but work, money and children.

Hugs, kisses and unexpected telephone calls to say "I love you." make the relationship strong. I suggest five touch points a day for one week - any kind gesture that takes 30 seconds or less. If a man can do this for his partner for one week, both will be amazed at how much better they feel in the relationship.

Romance is often associated with the initial days of courtship and dating. It seems to fly out of the window once couples start living together or get married. We human beings are tactile creatures and a loving touch or a cuddle goes a long way. If you're going for a hug, you have quite a few options – a loving embrace, a bear hug or those 'I never want to let you go' ones! A kiss can say more than a thousand words whether it is a peck on the cheek.

Express yourself by saying 'I love you' often (and mean it). Put it down on paper by writing a little love note and slip it into your partner's wallet, bag and pocket.

Plan a romantic get-away. Escape from the monotony and routine of everyday life and make the effort to spend some quality time together.

Take a walk on the beach, watch a movie together; whether it's a comedy or a romance, and share a bowl of popcorn.

Action movies and thrillers aren't exactly conducive to handholding. Complement each other. It's important to make each other feel good. If you like his new haircut or she's looking great, tell them so. Buy him/her a gift, Play game together. Turn up at her workplace to take her out to lunch. Women; wear sexy lingerie

Men, don't ever beat your wife for any reason. Prov. 19:11, Prov. 20:3. Don't ever forget that your wife is your greatest asset. Prov. 12:4, Prov. 18:22. Don't ever forget to check the level of peace of your wife. Prov. 27:17. Don't associate with men that lack credibility and generational mindset. Prov.13:20.

Don't ever hurt your wife no matter the level of insults passed on you. Col. 3:19, 1Pet.2:19-20. Don't ever wave off the ideas, advice or suggestions of your wife because of your selfish interest. Pro. 1:5, Pro.19:20. Never treat your wife as a servant. Eph. 5:29. Never make your wife a negative case study before friends and family. Prov. 5:18, Prov. 21:23Never doubt your wife no matter what you know about her past. 1Cor. 13:5.

Don't deny your wife of sex. 1Cor.7:4-5. Don't be careless about the welfare of your home. 1Tim. 5:8. Don't compare your wife with anyone. 2Cor.10:12. Never cheat on your wife no matter the condition. Prov. 6:32, Prov. 5:20. Never cut short the love you showed to your wife, rather, water it, and nurture it for effective continuous growing. Eph. 5:28-29

Never disregard the effort of your wife, rather appreciate her more and more. Prov. 31:28b. Never discuss the weak points of your wife at public opinion polls. Prov. 5:17. Don't call your wife unpleasant names such as prostitute, witch, fruitless entity, harlot, useless wife, bastard, rather call her blessed, precious, capable, beautiful and virtuous woman. Col. 4:6, Prov. 31:28-29.

Never ever place your friends, family or work above your wife. Don't be self centered. Eph. 5:28, Phil. 2:3-4. Don't ever cook up plans against your wife because of your lustful desires. Never set up a family without having a family vision. Prov. 29:18, Hab. 2:2-3.

Never make your wife feel inferior and uneducated before your friends, family, anyone or even you the husband. Never compare your wife's attitude with your one time girlfriend's attitude. 2Cor.10:12.

Don't be lazy to cater for your wife and family. 1Tim. 5:8. Never allow money to be the bond of love in your marriage. 1Tim. 6:10. Never allow your parents or family members to dictate the affairs of your home, remember, ''therefore shall a man leave his father and mother and cleave to his wife.........''. Gen. 2:23-24.

Don't ever let your children come between you and your wife. You married your wife not your children, remember they have their life to live and when married and gone, only your wife will still be with you, to cook for you, comfort you, refresh your body, soul and spirit in the bedroom. Matt. 19:6.

Never hide any phone calls, text messages, or password to mailbox from your wife. Transparency is the ultimate key to continuous trust and confidence in marriage. Rom. 12:9-10. Never owe your wife anything, always give her the very best; best in love, best care, most precious things and that which belongs to her. Rom.13:8.

Never show a heart of ungratefulness to God and your precious wife, always and always be ever grateful for their presence in your life. Prov. 31:28b

Bedrock 4: WHY HOMES BREAK

Little foxes that destroy marriages and families

Marriage is the oldest human institution.
It was instituted and commissioned by God Himself. In Genesis 2:18, 24, the bible records:
And the LORD God said, it is not good that the man should be alone; I will make him an help meet for him.
Therefore shall a man leave his father and his mother, and shall cleave unto his wife: and they shall be one flesh.

It is the intention of God for marriages to be fruitful and successful according to Genesis 1:27 – 28:
So God created man in his own image, in the image of God created he him; male and female created he them.
And God blessed them, and God said unto them, Be fruitful, and multiply, and replenish the earth, and subdue it: and have dominion over the fish of the sea, and over the fowl of the air, and over every living thing that move upon the earth.

God want families to live together in unity, peace and harmony. Psalms 133:1 However, marriage (families) faces both internal and external challenges. Some of these challenges are small in nature but very destructive.

It is important for us to understand what causes broken homes, so that we can guide against them in our families. For those who are already victims, they will be able to see where they missed it and make necessary amends with the help of God. For the unmarried, they would have understood what things to watch out for in their plans towards marriage.

Broken hearts produce broken homes or failed marriages and failed marriages lead to troubled lives. Moreover, since a bad tree cannot produce good fruits, children from broken homes are usually bad children.

Broken homes start with broken hearts. The bible says, "A merry heart doeth good like a medicine, but a broken spirit dried the bones" Pro. 17:22. Before physical separation can occur, spiritual separation would have taken place. None is good because they result in loss of focus and they detach us from God's purpose for our lives. The ministry of healing the broken hearted has been committed to us Isa. 61:11, and we must resist every move to be an instrument in the hand of the devil to break hearts. As couples, watch out for the following:

Intolerance, insensitivity, undue interference from the extended family, covetousness and irresponsibility are some of the reasons why we have broken homes.

Also wrong foundation may be another reason for broken home.
If the marriage is build on falsehood, the possibility of the marriage crash landing prematurely is very high

Sex and infertility may be another factors that may bring about broken home, couples with this is the fact that either of the couple may not be able to satisfy the other partners which may result in complaint and infertility

Problems may also arise when one partner has more decision-making power than that other in the finance of the family. When one person makes all the decisions about activities, friends, financial matters, household matters and vocations, such a relationship can become unstable. Both partner should equally share the decisions- making power

Don't invite outsider or third party into your personal affair. Any time you a quarrel or misunderstanding with your spouse make sure you settle it within yourselves. Don't expose your Nakedness to outsiders.

Barrenness, family planning. Care in labour, sex of babies, etc. Can break homes if not manage.
Rely on God, you need to take proper care of your home, entertain and respect any member of your husbands family and when this not done properly, home break.

Bad communication may lead to the home breaking Husband don't ever says "you will sol go to your father's house, to your wife. Every war can be manage with good communication.
Past mistakes must be explained and corrected with wisdom. Proverbs 15:1+23. &16:24 &25:11-15.

Excessive jealousy in relationships may lead home breaking. Jealousy is cited as one of the most frequent causes of Break-up of romantic relationships. Jealousy can trigger abuse and violence, which can cause a relationship to breakup

Age difference and egoism may lead to break up in home.
Agape love will make you to sacrifice to satisfy your pat.
When there is love, there will be fellowship. Appreciate him or her more than anyone else. If there is anything you discover after marriage, pretend as if it does not exit at all because you can not change your spouse in a day.

Break-up sign

1. You're always craving for time alone
2. You don't go out together anymore

3. You prefer seeing your friends to seeing your partner
4. You've stopped having Sex
5. You've stopped touching each other
6. You've stopped kissing
7. He/she no longer make you laughs
8. You don't chat anymore
9. You do all the chores
10. You've stopped liking yourself

Bedrock 5: SEX IN MARRIAGE

Have you ever wondered why God carefully positioned a membrane of blood in a lady's sexual opening? It is a tiny membrane that partially or completely covers the opening of the vagina. It is called the "HYMEN". Why would God-Our Maker put a breakable tissue full of blood at the very door of the sexual opening of the female?

It was God (our creator) who set that blood- filled vessel there as a covenant blockage, a sign and a token of a covenant between the bearer and whoever plunges into her opening.

Before God, to be dis-virgin is not a casual act of fun. It is a serious covenant. This is God's way of saying, "Whoever plunges into this woman shall only be able to do so by making a blood covenant to be joined to her for the rest of his life, from that point onward.

Little wonder why sexual intercourse was designed by God to take place only and only after the marriage contract is sealed. The one who made the body (the hormones, organs, nerves, tissues, e.t.c) said it in clear terms in 1Cor.6:13, *"Now, the body is not for fornication"*. Anyone who chooses to use the body for fornication must know that he/she is working directly against God's plan and there would definitely be a consequence either now or at old age.

There is a spiritual bonding, a supernatural process that takes place in a lady's heart to the first man that enters in to her especially at that particular time when the hymen breaks. There is no covenant without blood: this is why the membrane contains enough of it. As a matter of fact, what happen the first time a lady have sex is not just sex but an immersion and a bathing of the man with her hymen blood to initiate a covenant that is highly recognized in the spirit realm of both light and darkness. The first time this happens just marks her opening day covenant ceremony and each subsequent experience goes on to further refresh or strengthen that covenant or establish another version of it with another person.

Many have washed useless boys with that hymen-blood.
Many have struck irreversible covenants with men that have nothing to do with their destiny. Many have shared that hymen blood in sexual activity with demon-possessed men. If only they knew, many girls who carelessly allowed themselves to be dis-virgin in a bid to be among the so called "big girls" would never have done so.

The Bible says it in clear terms: "Or do you not know that he who is joined to a harlot (through sexual activity) is one with her (1 Cor. 6:16). This is why many girls are not yet married; their spiritual composition is already shattered and imbalanced, because they have mingled their souls with that of different men.

Dear Singles, know today that there is a definite proportion of your virtue that leaves you each time a man enters into you and when that man leaves you, he leaves with it. Just imagine how much of yourself would be lost each time a man enters into you without any properly signed marriage bond or contract.

Sex is a spiritual affair; a giving of yourself to another. All of these things have strong and terrible spiritual implications. A broken hymen opens you up to the spirit of the man that broke it, any other spirit whatsoever that may have mingled with that man's spirit, those who have mingled theirs with him and the spirit of any other man that enters into you thereafter. The fun part of pre- marital sex is not really funny. What happens in between the lines could be deadly and dangerous. HIV is just one among many of those demons of darkness sent to inflict pain on those who practice unauthorized and casual sex. Be careful.

A healthy sex life

It is important to understand that sex in itself is a pure and holy act created by God. It was made for the husband-wife relationship in order to ensure the perpetuation of the human race, and on the other, to deepen the husband and wife relationship.

The appetite for sex is something that was put within us by God. It is not dirty or evil in itself. The sex drive was God's idea not ours. In other words, He created those hormones that ginger us towards the opposite sex.

Sex, as God intended, should be beautiful when practiced legitimately within the confines at the institutions of marriage. Nothing ever created could be otherwise! The sex drive is not sinful when you are able to control it. It is a desire that can be put under subjection. However, the word "SEX" sounds irritating to some people. Many Christians today shy away from it;

When you're in the mood, it's a sure bet that the last thing on your mind is boosting your immune system or maintaining a healthy weight. Yet good sex offers those health benefits and more. That's a surprise to many people, says Joy Davidson, PhD, a New York psychologist and sex therapist.

Of course, sex is everywhere in the media, she says. "But the idea that we are vital, sexual creatures is still looked at in some cases with disgust or in other cases a bit of embarrassment. So to really take a look at how our sexuality adds to our life and enhances our life and our health, both physical and psychological, is eye-opening for many people."

Sex does a body good in a number of ways, according to Davidson and other experts. The benefits aren't just anecdotal or hearsay -- each of these 28 health benefits of sex is backed by scientific scrutiny.

Sex is also good for your health. Many people simply enjoy a healthy sex life because sex is pleasurable. Good sexual health can improve your physical health. An active sex regimen, a prescription of 2-3 times per week, has fascinating and evidenced-based benefits.

Enjoying a rigorous romp can do wonders for everyone both physically and psychologically. Therefore if sex has become a non-priority in your life, you may want to reconsider putting it at the top of your “to do” list, because not only could sex result in stronger teeth, it could actually save your life.

The following are different reasons why sex and sexual activity may help you live a longer, happier life due to the health benefits of sex:

Sexual activity is a form of physical exercise, “according to Dr. Michael Cirigliago of University of Pennsylvania school of medicine. Making love three times a week burns around 7,500 calories in a year—equivalent of jogging 75 miles.

A night of love can raise the amount of oxygen in cell, help in to keep organs and tissues functioning at their peak.

Any kind of physical exercise is going to increase testosterone, states Dr. Karen Donahue, director of sex and marital therapy programme at Chicago’s north-western

University medical centre. Testosterone is believed to help keep men's bones and muscles strong.
Making love regularly can lower levels of the body's total cholesterol slightly, while positively changing the ratio of good-to-bad cholesterol.

Sex can lower levels of "arthritic pain, whiplash pain and headache pain, "according to Dr. Beverly Whipple, precedent –elect of the American Association of Sex Education, counsellor and therapist. Hormones that are released during excitement and orgasm elevate pain thresholds.
DHEA (Dehydroepiandrosterone), a popular supplemental hormone, is released naturally during lovemaking. 'just before orgasm and ejaculation, 'DHEA spikes to levels three to times higher than usual'

Researchers say prostate trouble may arise or be worsened by fluid build-up within the gland. Regular ejaculation will help wash out those fluids. Be cautious when suddenly changing frequency –sudden changes may also trigger prostate problems.
Regular lovemaking can increase a woman's estrogen level, protect her heart and keep her vaginal tissues more supple, state Donahey.
Sex can be a very effective way of reducing stress level. A big health benefit of sex is lower blood pressure and overall stress reduction.

Sex boosts immunity. Good sexual health may mean better physical health. Having sex once a week has been linked with higher level of an antibody called immunoglobulin A or lgA, which can protect you from getting colds and other infections.
Sex burns calories. Thirty minutes of sex burns 85 calories or more. It may not sound like much, but it add up: 42 half-hour sessions will burn 3,570 calories, more than enough to lose a

pound. Doubling up, you could drop that pound in 21 hour-long sessions. Sex is a great mode of exercise.
Sex improves cardiovascular health. Sex twice r more a week reduced the risk of fatal heart attack.

Sex boost self-esteem. Boost self-esteem was one of the reasons people have sex. One of the reasons people say they have sex is to feel good about themselves.
Sex boost affection. Crenshaw says affectionate touch will increase levels of oxytocin –the 'bonding hormone. ''Oxytocin is a desire-enhancing chemical secreted by the pituitary.
Regular oxytocin release may hele courage frequent lovemaking.

Having sex and orgasms increases levels of the hormones oxytocin, the so-called love hormones, which helps us bond and build trust. Researchers from university of Pittsburgh and University of North Carolina evaluated 59 premenopausal women before and after warm contact with their husbands and partners ending with hugs. They found that the more contact, the higher the oxytocin levels.

Oxytocin allows us to feel the urge to nature and to bond, 'Britton says. Higher oxytocin has also been lined with a feeling of generosity. So if you are feeling suddenly more generous toward your partner than usual, credit the love hormone.

Sex reduces pain. As the hormone oxytocin urges, endorphins increase, and pain declines. So if your headache, arthritis pain or PMS symptoms seem to improve after sex, you can thank those higher oxytocin levels.
Sex reduces prostate cancer risk. Frequent ejaculation, especially in some men say around 20, may reduce the risk of prostate cancer.

Sex strengthens pelvic floor muscles. For women, doing a few pelvic floor muscle exercise known as Kegel exercises during sex offers a couple of benefits.
You will enjoy more pleasure, and you will also strengthen the area and help to minimize the risk of incontinence latter in life. To do a basic Kegel exercise, tighten the muscles of pelvic floor, as if you are trying to stop the flow of urine. Count to three, then release.

Sex helps you sleep better. The oxytocin released during orgasm also promotes sleep, according to research. Getting enough sleep has been linked with a host of other good things, such as maintaining a healthy weight and blood pressure. Something to think about; especially if you've been wondering why your guy can be active one minute and snoring the next.

Sex keep our skin young and healthy. Sex increases blood circulation, which helps pump oxygen to our skin resulting in a brighter appearance. Scientific tests find that when woman make love they produce amount of hormone oestrogen, which make hair shiny and skin smooth.

Sex fights cavities. Turns out that semen is shock-full of zinc, calcium and other tooth decay-fighting minerals that benefit us when our bodies absorb it. Also kissing each day will keep the dentist away. Kissing encourages saliva to wash food from the teeth and lowers level of the acid that causes decay, preventing plaque build-up. Sex can result in stronger teeth; it could actually save your life.

Reasons why we should not have sex outside of marriage

There's something very special about a couple's first time. In this physical act the two become one flesh. Yet it is more than just physical oneness — a spiritual union takes place. God planned for this exclusive experience of discovery and pleasure to happen only within the intimacy of marriage. If we don't wait, we miss out on a very special blessing from God. According to 1 Corinthians 6:16; *Sex is as much spiritual mystery as physical fact. As written in Scripture, "The two become one." Since we want to become spiritually one with the Master, we must not pursue the kind of sex that avoids commitment and intimacy, leaving us lonelier than ever—the kind of sex that can never "become one."* The Message)

If we live as carnal Christians, we will seek to gratify the desires of the flesh and live only to please ourselves. If we live this way, the Bible says we cannot please God. We will be miserable under the weight of our sin. As we continue to feed our fleshly desires, our spirit will grow weak and our relationship with God will be destroyed. Complacency with sin leads to worse sin, and eventually, spiritual death. The bible tells us in Romans 8:8, 13: *those controlled by the sinful nature cannot please God. For if you live according to the sinful nature, you will die; but if by the Spirit you put to death the misdeeds of the body, you will live.*

This one is a no-brainer. If we refrain from sex outside of marriage, we will be protected from the risk of catching sexually transmitted diseases. The bible also record in 1 Corinthians 6:18*: Run from sexual sin! No other sin as clearly affects the body as this one does. For sexual immorality is a sin against your own body.* (NLT)

One reason God tells us to honour marriage and keep the marriage bed pure has to do with baggage. We carry baggage into our sexual relationships. Memories from the past, emotional scars and unwanted mental images can defile our thoughts and make the marriage bed less than pure. Certainly God can forgive the past, but that doesn't mean we're free from the baggage that can linger in our minds. Let us consider what Hebrews 13:4 *says: Marriage should be honoured by all and the marriage bed kept pure, for God will judge the adulterer and all the sexually immoral.*(NIV)

Bedrock 6: CAUSES AND CURE FOR INFERTILITY

Infertility is the inability of a (married) couple to have children after having regular sex for at least one year.
Infertility is categorized in these two types:
Primary infertility which refers to those men/women who has never been pregnant or impregnated.

Secondary infertility is another form in which a woman had a child or children before, but currently she cannot conceive because of some medical, emotional or physical issues.
It has been found that a large number of women become infertile within their reproductive ages and they do not know about it.

The fertility rate of those that marry between the ages of 20-26 years is higher than those that marry between 32-40 years. In Nigeria alone, studies show that about 1 in 5 couple are infertile. Health, age and lifestyle are the major factor that causes infertility in women

INFERTILITY IN WOMEN.
It has been found that in women, the conception rate during intercourse IS ABOUT

THE KEYS TO DEAL WITH CHILDLESSNESS

Zachariah was faced with this predicament and Elizabeth his wife was childless, but even worse was the fact that they had become very old. In fact, the scripture states that she was called barren. As far as man was concerned it was over for her, but definitely not with God.

Like every other day in his life, he woke up one morning expecting the usual, but got the extraordinary. God had sent an angel with the incredible news that he would have a son, and not just a son the forerunner of our Lord Jesus Christ.
Isn't it amazing that what human beings consider as delay usually ends up bringing out the best of God in our situations. I perceive that the best conceivable is about to manifest for you in Jesus name!

There are some things to note, though, in the life of Zachariah what we naturally consider as "Waiting period", involves two key steps not too obvious to many.

He was a man of Prayer**.** All through the period of waiting he must have been given to regular prayers knowing that until it is over, one more prayer will always bring about the desired result. In other words, don't give up on praying. Pray until it happens. No wonder the angel's comment was "Don't be afraid for Your Prayer is heard". Now, I don't know what you have been praying about, today God is saying this to you: your prayer has been answered.

He was faithful. In spite of his unmet expectations, he remained faithful. He observed his duties consistently as a priest. In fact, the angel met Zachariah while he was serving in the synagogue. The truth is faithfulness is one sure key to God's abundant blessings. God always rewards faithfulness!

Bedrock 7: BREAKING FINANCIAL HARDSHIP IN MARRIAGE

Let us critically look at the account recorded in 2 Kings 4:1-8:

Now there cried a certain woman of the wives of the sons of the prophets unto Elisha, saying, Thy servant my husband is dead; and thou knowest that thy servant did fear the LORD: and the creditor is come to take unto him my two sons to be bondmen.

And Elisha said unto her, what shall I do for thee? Tell me, what hast thou in the house? And she said, Thine handmaid hath not anything in the house, save a pot of oil. Then he said, go, borrow thee vessels abroad of all thy neighbour, even empty vessels; borrow not a few.

And when thou art come in, thou shalt shut the door upon thee and upon thy sons, and shalt pour out into all those vessels, and thou shalt set aside that which is full. So she went from him, and shut the door upon her and upon her sons, who brought the vessels to her; and she poured out.

Poverty is defined by Webster's dictionary as "the state of one who lacks a usual or socially acceptable amount of money or material possessions".

By this definition, there will always be some level of poverty because unless everyone has an equal share, someone will have a less than the "usual" or "socially" acceptable amount. Note the key word in the definition is "socially". I point this out because poverty is becoming more of a social stigma which cannot be cured by welfare programs alone.

Poverty is a state of mind, one of not being as worthy as others. Poverty does not only affect those that are broke, it can also affect people who appear to be rich. For example, there are millionaires who still do not feel that they have enough or as much as they should have. This is poverty consciousness.

Poverty is passed on from generation to generation not through genes but can be passed by parents subconsciously teaching their children that there is no way out of poverty. Parents would not consciously teach their children to live in poverty. However, learning by example is a way most children learn and unless parents are consciously teaching their children ways to escape from being poor by seeking opportunities through taking responsibility, getting an education and increasing self-esteem, their children may be picking up the sign that this is all about life for them.

By parents falling victims of the mind-set that this is all what life has for them, they pass this on to their children as well. So poverty has less to do with what type of education one receives in school but rather what type of education is received at home about life.

To overcome poverty, the focus needs to be on one's state of mind. That is- teaching the mind a new thought pattern to overcome poverty consciousness. The key elements are:

One can be broke and feel prosperous. There are a few homeless people who want to live the life that they do because they have everything that they need (food and shelter) without the worry of working for material possessions. Many of us would shun the life of the homeless due to the implications of poverty. Yet, it is our own state of mind that influences what we see and feel rather than how others see us whether it is as a millionaire or as homeless.

Money is generated based on what we give the world whether it is via our labour (time), our creativity (intellect) or our investment (money). Money is a symbol of what we have sown on earth. Money flows to those who use their energy to make things happen. Many millionaires got to where they are from a lot of hard work and creativity.

It takes energy to get a good education that will pay off later. And, the investment in your future can be in a form other than just getting a high school or college education. A friend of mine who went into the military after school now works for a computer software company. He did it by investing time learning how to develop websites and starting his own business with a friend. Having this ambition showed his current employer how well qualified he was even without a college education and he got the job.

To avoid being financially bankrupt in your marriage:

> Don't worry about money but plan and apply the principle (Always make budget). Determine to be debt free (Don't go in deliberate debt, live below your income and list your debt and start paying from the list), evaluate your regular consumption bill, sell every useless assets plan and spend within your budget.

"IT IS BETTER TO TRUST IN THE LORD THAN TO PUT CONFIDENCE IN MAN
Psalm 118:8

Bedrock 8: SIMPLICITY IN DRESSING

Dress or appearances causes lots of disputes in the marriage, Some dress like slave, immature, shabby, Dress to kill, to attracts, to seduces, arrogance, harlots, masquerade, too extravagance or improper. Etc.
How do you dress, why did you dress that way and if Christ returns will you go with Him like this?

God is the first fashion designer but what is God intension? Don't let dress be your worry. Do your dress portray your salvation? When you dress, put on righteousness of God.

In Joshua 7:21, loss of fashion and dress lead Achan to steal and brought calamity to Israel. Evangelize unbeliever through your dressing. Righteousness is our spiritual garment that can give us access to God

Dress the way you want to be addressed
How you are dressed determines how you are received or treated. Your dressing is a part of your identity. How you dress equally affects your Kingdom walk.

If everyone in your environments is blind we you still dress that way?

Bedrock 9: TEN LIES THAT LEADS TO DIVORCE

If you and your partner stay intimately connected to God, your marriage will reflect that intimacy. Divorce doesn't have to happen. Recognize the cultural lies that influence you and counteract them with biblical truth. No marriage is beyond the probability of divorce but you can be proactive in preventing it. It's time to improve on the divorce statistics and divorce proof your marriage.

Lie 1: Marriage is a contract
Yes, marriage is a legal contract, but in God's eyes it is much more. The truth is marriage is a covenant, an unbreakable promise. It is life commitment, it means "for better for worse", richer or poorer, in sickness and in health"

Lie 2: I married you, not your family
The truth is you don't marry just your spouse; you get her family as a package deal! Don't kid yourself and think the outlawed in-laws don't matter. Your spouse grew up in a family that taught her how to be who she is today.

Lie 3: I can change my spouse
Wrong! The fact that she's continually late or her apartment is a mess is not likely to change because of your undying love. Pat attention to the red flags you see during the dating relationship, especially the more serious ones, such as drinking too much, violent temper, promise breaking, etc. Chances are these things won't improve but worsen after the honeymoon is over. The truth; all you have control over is your reaction to your spouse. That's the only part you can change.

Lie 4: We are too different

Differences are not a major problem as long as the differences are not about life values and morals. Incompatibility doesn't kill a relationship. The real issue is how you handle your differences. You need compatible styles that work for both people. Some differences are unsolvable and couples need to learn to accept those.

Lie 5: I've lost that loving feeling and it's gone, gone, gone!

Intense passion doesn't last forever but love can stay for a lifetime. You may not always feel love but you must determine to love your partner as yourself. The loving feeling dwindles when couples lock into negative patterns that lead them away from each other. Criticism moves to contempt and highly defensive behaviour that eventually leads to emotional distance. The truth is you can restore that loving feeling with a number of changes.

Lie 6: A more traditional marriage will save us

Out of frustration, many men feel that if their relationship could be more like the Brady Bunch couple. Life would be happier. They are confused about gender roles and responsibilities. Submission is misunderstood and often abused concept God's intention for marriage.

Lie 7: I can't change-this is who I am: take it or leave it.

An unwillingness to change is rooted in rebellion. Change doesn't happen when you don't embrace it.

Lie 8: There's been an affair. We need to divorce

Affairs are serious and damaging but they are not beyond repair. If both spouse agree to try. There must be a commitment to cut off the affair, a tome of repentance, forgiveness and a rebuilding of the relationship. The covenant has been broken but can be restored if a couple chooses to do so. It's not easy but possible.

Lie 9: It doesn't matter what I do: God will forgive me
God will forgive you if you repent but it does matter what you do.

Lie 10: It's too broken
If you've given up, the future looks hopeless, you've grown apart, can't manage conflict, made a mistake or whatever the problem, believe that God can work when you can't. He can change hearts, do miracles and work in the most difficult circumstances. He is the God of the possible. Draw close to Him, intercede for your marriage, do battle with your true enemy (Satan) and expect God to work on your behalf.

A SILENT SERMON

Bro. Stephen and sis. Stella have been married for about three years. Sis. Stella is a worker in God's Vineyard (choir) but the husband is just a member. But this woman always nags and often quarrels with her husband. This continues for some time and the husband concluded to report her to the Reverend that faithful Saturday. The man pretended to keep her company to the Church for choir practice. By so doing he can report his wife to the Rev. Unfortunately, the Rev. was not around but on their way back home they branch at his residence. About to climb the staircase, they met the Rev. fighting his wife with the wife sustaining injuries from several knocks from the dining chair (kudos to the Rev.). They quickly carried her to the hospital. On their way home, the man (bro Stephen) said to his wife: I don't think this Rev.

qualifies to counsel us or intervene in our marital problems for our home is better than his.

THE POWER OF THREE LITTLE WORDS

Some of the most significant messages people deliver to one another often come in just three words. When spoken or conveyed, those statements have the power to forge new friendships, deepen old ones and restore relationships that have cooled.

The following three word phrases can enrich every relationship:

I'LL BE THERE - Being there for another person is the greatest gift we can give.

I MISS YOU - Perhaps more marriages could be salvaged and strengthened if couples simply and sincerely said to each other, "I miss you." This powerful affirmation tells partners they are wanted, needed, desired and loved.

I RESPECT YOU - Respect is another way of showing love. Respect conveys the feeling that another person is a true equal. It is a powerful way to affirm the importance of a relationship.

MAYBE YOU'RE RIGHT - This phrase is highly effective in diffusing an argument and restoring frayed emotions. The flip side of "maybe you're right" is the humility of admitting "maybe I'm wrong".

PLEASE FORGIVE ME - Many broken relationships could be restored and healed if people would admit their mistakes and ask for forgiveness. we should never be ashamed to admit our mistakes.

I THANK YOU - Gratitude is an exquisite form of courtesy. People who enjoy the companionship of good, close friends are those who don't take daily courtesies for granted.

COUNT ON ME - "A friend is one who walks in when others walk out." "Loyalty is an essential ingredient for true friendship; it is the emotional glue that bonds people. Those who are rich in their relationships tend to be steady and true friends. When troubles come, a good friend is there, indicating "you can count on me".

LET ME HELP - The best of friends see a need and try to fill it. When they spot a hurt they do what they can to heal it.

I UNDERSTAND YOU - People become closer and enjoy each other more if they feel the other person accepts and understands them. Letting others know in so many little ways that you understand him or her is one of the most powerful tools for healing your relationship.

GO FOR IT - Some of your friends may be non-conformists, have unique projects and unusual hobbies. Support them in pursuing their interests. Rather than urging your loved ones to conform, encourage their uniqueness everyone has dreams that no one else has.

I suppose the 3 little words that you were expecting to see have to be reserved for those who are special; that is **I LOVE YOU**.

Bedrock 10: TURN YOUR HOUSE TO HOME

House is what you build or bay within your money but home is what you made with commitments, dedication, endurance and responsibility.
Home is the habitation of family or habitation were family dwell together, the starting point of every destiny, ministry, carrier and long life

And the Lord God said, it is not good that the man should be alone; I will make him an help meet for him. And out of the ground the Lord God formed every beast of the field, and every fowl of the air, and brought them unto Adam to see what he would call them: and whatsoever Adam called every living creature that was the name thereof. And the rib, which the Lord God had taken from man, made him a woman, and brought her unto the man. And Adam said this is now bone of my bones, and flesh of my flesh: she shall be called Woman, because she was taken out of Man. Therefore shall a man leave his father and his mother, and shall cleave unto his wife: and they shall be one flesh. Gen. 2.18-24.

One crazy thing married people do today is for a man to get married, and stay in his father's house and his mother's house with that wife.
This is contrary to the scripture. Such marriages normally run into trouble.

The house is not the home. You could have a beautiful house but no home inside. The real home is built by man and woman join together in marriage and their children. The home is a foundation of a strong nationhood. The more reason the devil does not like the home at all. The devil knows that if he can successfully penetrate the home and destroy the home, the nation is destroyed. The naked truth is that, the devil has achieved a great success in this regard. That is why we found a lot of strange things happen.

If you, as a child of God, marry a child of the devil, the devil becomes your father in-law and to have the devil as a father in-law is a terrible father in-law indeed.
Because that devil hates marriage with perfect hatred. He knows that two are better than one.

And he doesn't want them to unite. He knows that it is not good for a man to be alone. So he wants to use the loneliness and destroy the man. He knows that God loves marriage. He wants to destroy the marriage, because he hates everything God loves.

And you must resolve it. The devil has entered into that marriage and you must chase them out. The devil wants confusion in our world. And the way to cause confusion is to confuse marriages. The devil knows that when two gather in the name of the Lord, he doesn't want those two to be together. The devil knows that marriage brings strength. He doesn't want that strength. The devil knows that a good marriage leads to prosperity.

He doesn't want that prosperity. The devil knows that a good marriage would raise godly children. He doesn't want those Godly children. The devil knows that a vibrant happy powerful church is just a group of happy vibrant powerful family homes. The devil knows that a good marriage leads to a peace of mind. He doesn't want people to have that peace. The devil knows that Godly sex is only permitted inside marriage. He doesn't want that, so that people will be having ungodly sex and destroy their life. The devil knows that the best thing to destroy in the life of a child is to destroy the marriage of his or her parents. So the devil is not a friend of marriage.

Unfortunately, a lot of people go to marriages with all kinds of expectations. We asked a lady "what do you expect in your marriage?" she said sir, I expect my husband to take of me and pamper me. I expect my husband to help me in the kitchen. I expect my husband to help me baby sir, when I'm busy. I expect my husband to meet my financial needs. I expect my husband to always listen to me and respect me always. I expect my husband to be at home latest 6.00 p.m. I expect plenty of romance in my marriage.

We asked a man too, what do you expect in your marriage? He said I expect my wife to cook all my food because I hate cooking. I expect sex 6 times in a week. I expect my wife to support my family with money. I expect my wife not to worry if she sees me with any woman, or women sending me messages. I expect my wife to stop sending my clothes to dry-cleaners and wash the clothes.

So the expectation of the lady is different from the expectation of the man. There is a problem.
Marriage is a game of two people who have decided to make things work.

Most people get married believing a myth that marriage is a box full of all the things they have longed for: companionship, intimacy, friendship etc. The truth is that marriage at the start is an empty box. You put something in before you can take anything out. There is no love in marriage. Love is in people. And people put love in marriage. There is no romance in marriage. You have to infuse it into your marriage. A couple must learn the art and form the habit of giving, loving, serving, praising, keeping the box full.
If you take more than what you give it become empty

There are some crazy things that happen too, which should not be found in a Christian home:
Rejection of food cooked by your wife because you're angry. Rejecting the food that was cooked with your money. You are a man telling your wife over and over again, "get this into your thick head, I am the head of this family do you understand?" Shouting on your wife. Issuing threat of divorce at any slight provocation. Beating the wife or leaving the house. They are crazy things some couples do.

Each time they start, the devil begins to open praise worship section. When a man is keeping malice with his wife, he is keeping diaries of offenses. Abusing the wife and criticizing the wife. Accusing the wife that had two to three children, that she is now a witch. Mother-in-law witch, father-in-law wizard. Everybody is now a witch, fighting the wife on the street.

I remember one of my father in Lord in those days. He said the day he stopped fighting his wife at home was the day they were fighting and one man knocked the door. The best drunkard on the street. He said, "Pastor so not only drunkards like us do beat women." He said, "so you're a drunkard too, only that you don't drink beer. You are beating madam, I'm sorry for you." The drunkard walked out. That was the day the man stopped.

Calling your wife names, fool, goat, animal, double neck leg. The truth is, whatever you call your wife is what you are too. Because the Bible says two shall become one. Transferring your frustration at work on the woman at home. You watch your wife labouring herself to death at home, cooking, boiling etc. You just put your leg on the stool and watching the television. All you want or say bring my food here. All those are crazy things that people do in marriage and it is very sadden. Also it applicable to our sisters. When you hate your in-Laws. You're doing a boxing ring with your mother-in-law. You begin to dress very badly, after you have married and you say leaving the house dirty, unkempt is crazy. Refuse to cook because you're angry.

Challenging your husband to beat you. Employing beautiful fully grown female house help to be looking after your home when you're at work. You cannot cook and you refuse to learn how to cook. Not ready to lose any argument. Blaming your husband for anything wrong at home. Talking about your ex-boyfriends to your husband, how good they were, is madness. Shouting during a discussion.

So as far as the Bible is concerned, it is not only those who are in a psychiatric hospital who are mad. There are plenty of mad people on the street who don't take any drug, but who are crazy. This thing is annoying heaven. When the family don't pray together, it annoys heaven. In fact, the Bible says that God is against the family that did not pray together. (Jer. 10:25). So if you are in the category of these people that allow a little bit of madness creep into your marriage, chase the madness out and get together and unite, and see what the force of your unity can do in prayer.

"Any woman who still thinks marriage is a fifty-fifty proposition is only proving that she doesn't understand either men or percentages"

"The married state, with and without the affection suitable to it, is the completest image of heaven and hell we are capable of receiving in this life"

PRAYER POINTS

PRAYER FOR THE MARRIAGEABLE YOUTH AND SINGLE THAT IS SEARCHING FOR MR. /MRS. RIGHT

1. A little key opens a very big lock. From today in my life, every little effort will bring unusual success that will make your story glorious news.
2. All persistence and repeated struggle of my father house & spouse lineage that is manifest in me end today. Galatians 3:13-14
3. All repeated struggle of my family that is manifest in me end. Galati 3:13-14
4. Almighty God, cause every siege against my family to cease now. Let us begin to enjoy your abundant grace
5. Almighty God, cause every siege against my family to cease now. Let us begin to enjoy your abundant grace
6. Anything planted in my life to frustrate my marital life, come out now in the name of Jesus
7. As the north is far from the south. And sky is far from the ground evil, sorrow, weeping, death and calamities shall be far from your home in Jesus name.
8. As the womb of a woman co-operates with a God ordained baby so shall your life cooperate with the blessings and breakthroughs meant for you in Jesus name.
9. Ask Holy Ghost fire to consume every instrument of the devil in your life today
10. By the power of God on the day of my marital reward I will not be missing.
11. By the power of God, let every enemy of my home be disgraced and paralysed in Jesus Name.
12. Every anti-marriage curse uttered against my life by anyone, be broken in the name of Jesus.
13. Every arrow of rituals and sacrifices against my marriage back fire in the name of Jesus.

14. Every cobweb spirit attacking my marital life be roasted in the name of Jesus
15. Every elders in my family negotiating my marriage and breakthrough at the gate of my life die.
16. Every enemy of my full scale laughter, be destroyed in Jesus' name
17. Every evil agreement on my behalf between my parent and any one terminated by the blood of Jesus
18. Every evil finger pointed at me and my family, dry up never to function again in Jesus name
19. Every evil hand compassing your business causing disappointments, low sales, and debts.
20. Every evil hand compassing your life about causing delay, stagnation, unfruitfulness, unrighteousness, addictions and bitterness: today, in the name of Jesus Christ they are destroyed.
21. Every evil hand compassing your marriage causing lack, infidelity, instability and strife.
22. Every evil hand compassing your womb causing delay, failure. Every evil hand compassing your reproductive organs causing miscarriage, abortion and low sperm count.
23. Every evil hand manipulating my marital life and relationship, dry in Jesus Name
24. Every evil program designed by household witches for me, be cancelled in Jesus Name.
25. Every evil ring on my finger driving away my spouse is removed by fire in the name of Jesus.
26. Every evil spoken word against position ahead of your glorious Future l command them to collapse & God begins to accelerate your success Journey from 2day.
27. Every force that is overtaking my opportunity 2 success die. Job 5:12
28. Every force that is overtaking my opportunity loses your grip over me. Job 5:12
29. Every hidden voice speaking against my marital enjoyment, be silenced in Jesus Name

30. Every satanic committee, organized to disgrace me and my home, scatter in Jesus Name.
31. Every satanic investment in my marriage is wasted in the name of Jesus.
32. Every source that brings bitterness into your life would be dried off
33. Every spiritual marriage contesting for my physical marriage in the name of Jesus
34. Every strange power attempting to destroy my seat, receive the judgement of God in Jesus Name.
35. Every unknown curse, keeping me away from my spouse break in Jesus' name
36. Every wall between me and the visitation of God be broken in the name of Jesus
37. Every wicked prayers offered because of my seat be cancelled in the Name of Jesus.
38. Every wrong person sent into my life to delay my marital journey, be disgraced in Jesus' name
39. Evil candles and incense against my life and marriage back fire in Jesus name.
40. Father Anointing to Completely Break Long-Standing Barriers & Totally Destroy Satanic Yokes that have limited my marriage & work. ACT 10:38. Isa 10:27. Gala 6:17.
41. Father Anointing to Completely Break Long-Standing Barriers & Totally Destroy Satanic Yokes that have limited me as a local champion. ACT 10:38. Isaiah 10:27. Galatia 6:17
42. Father chase away evil beasts, tormentors and affliction from my home
43. Father every sanction pronounces upon me, my marriage be destroy father every stone roll against my marriage be remove matt. 28:2
44. Father give me peace in my home, take away everything that causes fear from my life
45. Father grant me victory over all my enemies

46. Father Lord, let every seed of the sickness in my life be uprooted by fire, by force in the name of Jesus.
47. Father Lord, terminate the life of all sickness in my life, in the name of Jesus.
48. Father Lord, your name is Jehovah Rapha, heal every infirmity in my life in the name of Jesus.
49. Father make me and my children fruitful, multiply us oh Lord and establish your covenant with us in Jesus mighty name
50. Father makes my vision of establishment acceptability & gain credibility with helper of my destiny. 1Chron 12:21-22
51. Father, destroy any bad seed in me that the devil is trying to water.
52. Father, let my good harvest in the remaining part of this year exceed all the harvest of my previous years put together.
53. Father, make me a Living Testimony.
54. Father, Multiply my good seeds and waters them by your hands.
55. Father, overthrown every demonic caretaker ruling my life, business and family affair. Isa 49:24-26
56. Father, release your fresh anointing upon me, anoint me to overflowing
57. Father, release your fresh anointing upon me, anoint me to overflowing
58. Holy Ghost fire burn to ashes every token of evil spiritual marriage in the name of Jesus
59. Holy Ghost, arise with your weapons of fire and give me my marital breakthrough this year in the name of Jesus
60. I blend all activities of spirits from the air, water, land and family idols, and I forbid them from interfering in my relationship from today in Jesus' name.
61. I Break Free From Every Manifestation of Limitation In My Marital life
62. I break the chain of marital stagnancy in the name of Jesus
63. I break the yoke of the spirits having access to my marital future in the name of Jesus

64. I bring fire from the altar of the Lord upon every evil marriage in the name of Jesus
65. I command every spirit of division to depart from us in the name of Jesus.
66. I command total deliverance upon my family, church, marriage, etc., from the stronghold of the mighty, in the name of Jesus.
67. I decree to your life that from this day, you will rise and ALL those who have been carrying you, you will begin to carry them in Jesus Name (amen).
68. I destroy all efforts of the enemy to frustrate my marriage, in the name of Jesus.
69. I dismantle any engagement with the spirit of death in the name of Jesus.
70. I forbid re-grouping and reinforcement of any evil against my marriage in Jesus name.
71. I Have Completely Broken Free from Every Manifestation of Limitation, Stagnation, Hindrances & Impediments Affecting Other People in My office & Marriage.
72. I overcome every ill health by the blood of Jesus and by the word of my testimony and faith, in the name of Jesus.
73. I overthrow every evil marital plan for my life in the name of Jesus
74. I overthrow every prince of Persia that is hindering my and marriage. giant breakthrough
75. I overthrow every prince of Persia that is hindering my and marriage. giant breakthrough
76. I rebuke every refuge of sickness in my life in the name of Jesus.
77. I recover myself and marriage from every evil diversion in the name of Jesus.
78. I redeem myself by the blood of Jesus from every sex covenant hindering my marital success in the name of Jesus
79. I refuse to be & redundant by the forces of wickedness, i also reject every satanic manipulation & agenda against my miracle. Jere .30:16-17

80. I renounce and divorce my marriage with the spirit husband/wife, in Jesus name
81. I renounce every conscious and unconscious familiar spirit and i reject your covenant, in the name of Jesus.
82. I renounce every inherited marital delay in Jesus name
83. I speak unto my umbilical gate to overthrow all negative parental spirits in the name of Jesus
84. I will not be sweep out of my marriage, position, in the name of Jesus.
85. In the name of Jesus wherever my spouse is begin to come in Jesus name.
86. In the Name of Jesus, I declare, no one will take my seat from me.
87. Isa 28:18. Colossians 2:14-15. Kings 13:4. Father let every hand of affliction stretched at me and my family wither now in Jesus name
88. Isa 30:21 - Father show me the way to go at every junction of life, don't let me miss d way
89. Jesus overthrew every demonic caretaker ruling my life & marriage affair.
90. Jesus said to the impotent man by the pool called Bethesda, "Rise, take up thy bed, and walk"
91. Jos 6:12. Isa 45:1-5+14:1-3. Every evil agreement on my name is terminate by d blood of Jesus
92. Let all activities contrary my wedding day be paralyzed in the name of Jesus
93. Let all anti-marriage yokes break in the name of Jesus Christ.
94. Let all spirits of fear , depression, worry and despair release me now in the mighty name of Jesus
95. Let all the effect of evil spiritual wedding rings, garments and shoes be completely removed in Jesus' name
96. Let any wicked spirit polluting the heart of my godly spouse-to-be against me receive the stones of fire in the name of Jesus.

97. Let every evil architect destroying my marriage plans be exposed and disgraced in Jesus name
98. Let every evil hand stretched forth to cover my marriage be cut off by the sword of fire of god in Jesus name.
99. Let every evil veil of hatred against me in the heart of my godly spouse be destroyed in the name of Jesus.
100. Let every family cage holding my godly spouse be destroyed by the fire of God in Jesus' name
101. Let the angel of God wipe off my name from the book of marital stagnancy in the name of Jesus
102. Let the counsel of God prosper in my life in the name of Jesus
103. Let the joy of the enemy over my marriage be converted to sorrow in the name of Jesus.
104. lord bring to light every darkness shielding my marriage potentials in the name of Jesus
105. Lord Jesus you are the yoke breaker, break every yoke of infirmity in my life, in the name of Jesus.
106. Lord Jesus, wash away every anti-marriage stamp, label and links from my life with your blood.
107. Lord let my Labour Attract Great Favour & My Activities Will Yield Increased Productivity from today. Psalm 71:21
108. Lord let my Labour Attract Great Favour & My Activities Will Yield Increased Productivity from today. Psalm 71:21
109. lord, advertise yourself as the living god in my life and marriage in the name of Jesus
110. Lord, let your anointing upon me and my family disgrace every stubborn pursuer of our lives
111. Lord, let your anointing upon me and my family disgrace every stubborn pursuer of our lives
112. Lord, reverse all evil curses issued against me and my marriage in Jesus name.
113. My father, my father, enough is enough, let my marital joy come in the name of Jesus
114. My God, you are God, my being alive is testifying that you are good in Jesus

115. My life will not follow any inherited evil marital pattern in the name of Jesus
116. My lord & my god raise pillar for my vision let it receive acceptability & gain credibility with helper of my destiny. 1chron 12:21-22
117. My miracle shall not be aborted
118. My Father, Let every cankerworm, palmer worm and caterpillar of disease in my life be roasted by fire by force in the name of Jesus.
119. No matter their number, let me triumph over them all
120. Oh lord , by your supreme power let my God given wife/husband locate me in Jesus' name
121. Oh Lord let every germs of infirmity in my life die, in the name of Jesus.
122. Oh Lord let my blood be transfused with the blood of Jesus.
123. Oh Lord Thank You because Your plan for my marriage will come to pass
124. Oh Lord, break every covenant that I made with infirmity in the name of Jesus.
125. Oh Lord, every dead organ receive life in the name of Jesus.
126. Oh Lord, I command death upon all sickness in my body in the name of Jesus.
127. Oh lord, I reject and renounce every spiritual marriage that is delaying my physical marriage in the name of Jesus
128. Oh Lord, in my life and destiny no one will take my position
129. Oh Lord, in my marriage, no one will take my position
130. Oh Lord, let every altar of darkness connect me to infirmity collapse and die in the name of Jesus.
131. Oh lord, let every evil cloud covering me be completely destroyed in the mighty name of Jesus.
132. Oh Lord, let every knee of infirmity in my life bow to the name of Jesus.
133. Oh Lord, let every pestilence of infirmity in my life die, in the name of Jesus.
134. Oh Lord, let every spirit hindering my healing die in the name of Jesus.

135. Oh lord, let every wrong spiritual odour repelling my future wife/husband is cancelled in Jesus' name.
136. Oh Lord, let the blood of Jesus flush out every satanic deposit in every area of my life, in the name of Jesus.
137. Oh Lord, let the desire of the enemy to cage my life with sickness be dashed to pieces in the name of Jesus.
138. Oh Lord, on the day of my marital joy, my seat will not be empty.
139. Oh lord, put the love for me back n the heart of my would-be spouse in the name of Jesus.
140. Oh lord, recreate my beauty to attract my God given partner in the name of Jesus
141. Oh lord, rent your heavens and deliver me to my husband and my husband to me in Jesus' name
142. Oh lord, wherever the bone of my bones is, begin to look for me in Jesus' name
143. overthrow every satanic strongman attached to my marriage and breakthrough
144. Pray against any power that the enemy is using against me
145. Pray for God to provide all the resources for your wedding. The miracle needed for you that day, after he has provided you a partner, pray to God to give it to you.
146. Pray that every power denying you of marriage. May God Almighty destroy them in Jesus name?
147. Pray that today shall begin your day of liberation
148. Ps 18:19 - Father by your grace bring me forth into a large place; deliver me according to your delight in me oh Lord
149. Ps 25:9 - Father guide me to make correct decision that will lead me to success in my career
150. Ps 37:23 - Father order my steps to where your divinely ordained blessings for me are located
151. Satan, i cancel your plan for my life, husband, children business and my marriage in Jesus name.
152. The 3 wise men did not REST, nor gave up until they found JESUS

153. The same flood that destroyed the world in Gen 7 lifted up the Noah ark. I decree every adversity of this world shall become your stepping stone to your breakthrough IN JSN.
154. those who shall BLESS you this season will not rest until they LOCATE you very soon
155. Thou spirit of delay, enough is enough, leave me now in the name of Jesus
156. Thou spirit of premature death, you will not take me away from my marital seat.
157. Uncommon Supernatural Advancement to overtake those that have outrun you receives now In Jesus name.
158. You pharaoh in my marriage, i bury you in the red sea in the name of Jesus.
159. You spirit of Egypt, release my marriage in the name of Jesus.
160. You spouse, you will not follow the evil patterns of any parent or ancestors n Jesus' name
161. You that power of darkness that planted sickness in my life, in my dream die in the name of Jesus.
162. Let every agents of impossibility fashioned against me receive permanent failure.

About the Book

Bedrock for wedlock is a *compendium for singles, searching, engaged, married and trouble how,* in this book discusses eleven powerful topics that deal with the foundation of marriage; why we Mary, who can we marry, how to know who to Mary, the processes of dating, courtside that lead to happy marriage, how to manage your marriage, why homes break, sex; finances; marriage, causes and cure for infertility, dressing, lies of divorce how to turn your house to a home with over 160 prayer points

About the Author

Joel Odunayo Daramola is the Pastor in Charge of Zone in the Christian Church of God, who God raised from grass to grace. He was a trained R & A Engineer (thermodynamic) with over 2 decades experience. He is the CEO AYO-TECHNICAL SERVICES (ATS). A publisher of the Monthly Journal: "VISION LINK" since 1999; a host of POWER SERVICE (revival, deliverance and breakthrough services)

He has a Vision to challenge young people to actualize their Potentials in life.

He is happily married to Pastor (Mrs.) C.O. Daramola and their union is blessed with four Children: Power, Queen, Excellence and Great

BB 5C0BEF8F. +2348033275896
Website. www.visionlink4u.org
pastordara@visionlink4u.org
pastordara@yahoo.com
visionlinkdara1@gmail.com

www.ingramcontent.com/pod-product-compliance
Lightning Source LLC
La Vergne TN
LVHW050317160826
845677LV00014B/3435

* 9 7 9 8 3 6 8 2 0 3 6 6 9 *